THE ROLE OF INDIGENEOUS MUSIC IN MODERN AFRICAN EDUCATION

A Uganda and East African setting

By

Mbabi-Katana

Dip.Ed. (E.A), LRAM, MA. (WSU), Ph.D. (Northwestern),
Professor of Music, Makerere University (1986 - 1991).

Pelican Publishers Ltd
P.O. Box 14232 Kampala,
Uganda.
Email: disingoma@pelicanpublishers.com
Website: www.pelicanpublishers.com

©**Mbabi-Katana**
Pelican Edition 2011

ISBN 9970 575 40 4

Preface

The title for this work is not the same as that originally conceived for a Dissertation written in partial fulfilment for the degree of Doctor of Philosophy, in the field of Music Education at Northwestern University. The alteration of the title was necessitated by the nature of the concepts, raised in this work, which command a universal African application.

The problems facing Music Education in Africa, while similar in nature, are numerous and varied when looked at on an African Continental plane. The Author has, therefore narrowed down the unit of study in this connection to one country, namely, Uganda.

The subject matter appearing in the course work[1] have been drawn from the entire East Africa and from some ethnic groups adjoining the borders of the main East African Countries of Uganda, Kenya and Tanzania.

It is the author's hope that this work which apart from dealing extensively with the subject of Music Education in Africa, and offering enormous opportunities in sideline studies will inspire serious investigations into issues raised in the work.

It is also his hope that the work will benefit not only educators but musicologists, anthropologists and various Africanists

MBABI-KATANA

---

1   Three separate volumes entitled Primary Music Course I, II and III were originally published by Uganda Publishing House. Now Music I is published by Fountain Publishers Ltd and II and III are published by Pelican Publishers Ltd.

ACKNOWLEDGEMENTS

For the quick and successful writing of this dissertation, the author is indebted to Dr. Clifton. A. Burmeister, Chairman, Department of Music Education, Northwestern University, who conscientiously supervised the preparation of this work.

The author wishes to record gratefully his indebtedness to the Rockefeller Foundation whose appropriation entitled 'Research and Training in African Music' granted to the former University of East Africa enabled the author to collect the data employed in the dissertation.

Finally, the author wishes to express his gratitude to his friends, Mr. G.P.K. Kakooza, Mrs. Florestee Vance and Mr. Lester Helmar Lashley, who assisted him in preparing the illustrations appearing in the coursework, and to Mr. P. Kirindi, who gave him permission to use his words to one of the songs in the course work.

Contents

TABLE OF ILLUSTRATIONS

1

Statement of the Problem

Conceived in this Dissertation is a curriculum based on a genuine philosophy, embodying indigenous cultural richness and diversity, and reflecting political, social and ethical values of the society of Uganda.

Geographical, historical, social, educational and philosophical aspects of the problem are fully discussed as a preamble to this Dissertation.

The Geographical Setting of Uganda

The State of Uganda epitomizes the beauty of Africa. In the East of the country towers Elgon Range. Westward lies the snow-covered Rwenzori Range, referred to as 'Mountain of the Moon' in the Ancient Egyptian legends. Southward lies Lake Victoria from which issues the River Nile, northward bound through the dry deserts of Sudan and Egypt to the Mediterranean Sea.

Uganda is a tropical country blessed with heavy rainfall and fertile soil, interspersed with good pasture lands. Consequently, agriculture forms a major occupation for the majority the inhabitants, and a substantial section of the population is engaged in animal husbandry. The entire population is predominantly rural and is likely to remain so for a long time. There are few towns in the country, and the urban population consists of Government Civil Servants, traders and a few industrial labourers.

Ethnically, Uganda is a focal point of the original major African races, namely, Hamites, Negroes and Pygmies. As a result of a long history of contact of these races and of their miscegenation, many racial variations have evolved. Such ethnic variety is reflected in cultural richness and diversity. The following description would emphasize the cultural and ethnic diversity of the people of Africa as well as their capacity for adaptability to change as reflected in the population of Uganda.

The significance of the Hamites in the composition of the African population consists in the fact that as nomads and as conquering warriors they have not confined themselves to their original homes, but have pushed their way into the countries of the Negroes. Owing to their racial superiority they have gained leading positions and have become the founders of many of the larger states in Africa. Their influence is strongest in East and South Africa and in the Sudan, i.e., the territory between the Sahara and the forest lands. Most of the peoples living in these regions are a result of crossing between Hamites and Negroes[2].

The majority of Hamites are cattle-owners, and this has no doubt intensified their racial qualities. The calling of herdsman leads man more into the loneliness of the wide steppes than the sociable life of the farmer. Owing to the constant necessity of protecting himself and his cattle against human and animal enemies, he is thrown upon his own resources. He must look for fresh pasturage, and often enough win it by conquest. He has little to lose, with the exception of his herds, which can easily be moved, and is therefore more inclined to settle disputes by war than is the sedentary Negro. The Hamite is proud, reserved, self-conscious, and warlike. He has accustomed himself to live as an aristocrat among the Negroes, and to look on them as his subjects. Their Chief occupation, agriculture, seems to him unworthy. Cattle's breeding is the only activity worthy of an aristocrat; Agriculture is left to the inferior classes. His relationship to the European is different also from that of the Negro. He does not see in the white man a superior being but a kinsman, and the Fulani addressed the first Europeans who came to them as cousins. This racial consciousness, which is quite natural to the Hamites, is still more marked in places where they have accepted Islam. As a rule they are indifferent or inimical to European civilization and education. It costs them a great effort of self-denial to admit the superiority of the white man, and to adapt themselves to the new conditions of life created by him. As economic values are more highly esteemed today than aristocratic privileges, they are in danger of being relegated to the background in comparison with the Negroes.

The Negroes are, apart from their mixture with other groups, a homogeneous race. Their division into Bantu and Sudan Negro is a linguistic one and not a racial distinction

2 Westermann, Diedrich. The African Today. London: Oxford University Press, 1934. pp. 26-27.

.... The Negro is physically well developed; his agriculture and his rich material culture have accustomed him to constant activity In contrast to the Hamite and Pygmy it was easy for him to adapt himself to the conditions of today.[3]

The Negro is a peasant; he loves the cultivation of the soil and in it finds his vocation............ Other occupations such as hunting and fishing, rearing cattle or plying a craft are only subsidiary to the agriculture which nourishes every household and is the foundation of all material life.[4]

The Pygmies are distinguished by their small stature. They have a light-coloured skin which is usually covered with light, downy hair. They are not sedentary, but move about as hunters and collectors, each group in a definite district, to which it claims a right of owner ship.................. They do not practice agriculture or possess cattle, but are dependent on what a day's roaming in bush or forest offers them.[5]

The pure original pygmy stock has almost completely disappeared from Uganda.

Traditional African Education

In Africa, as well as in many lands, the strength of the family is reflected in that of the society. It was the family in Africa that undertook the entire burden of providing, with devotion, the education of the young.

A family consists of several households in which live the head of the family, his wife or wives, their unmarried sons and daughters, as well as their married sons, their wives and children.

The Young Members have obligation to help or make presents to the older members, especially to the ranking member who carries the moral responsibility for their welfare.

---

3   ibid.
4   ibid.
5   ibid., p. 21.

The family ties are more often thought of as categorical than individual. Most terms of relationship are applied not to the individual but to a group of persons.[6]

Thus all members of the same generation within a clan[7] or group of related clans may call each other as brothers and sisters.

A child has to learn correct behavior to his relatives and his superiors in age. This makes him conscious of the fact that he is a member not only of his family but of a large group which in turn influence him to learn from his elders' knowledge and attitudes to life.

Education is not something which the African has received for the first time from the white man ....Many Africans, men and women, who have never been to school nor in contact with Europeans, show such dignified and tactful behavior, and reveal so much refinement in what they say and do that they well deserve to be called 'educated.' On the other hand, 'uneducated' behavior is at times met with among people who have for years been under intensive European influence and in schools conducted by Europeans.[8]

The term "education" in one of the most prominent Bantu languages is known as "Okugunjura,"[9] a word whose literal equivalent is English is "upbringing." Inherent in the meaning of this word is the act of preparing, training and transforming a young person into a mature responsible person.

Under the traditional African system, education took the form of socialization and maturation of children, and of inducting them into the accumulated heritage of their predecessors.

---

6   Moore Clark D. and Dunbar, Ann. Africa Yesterday and Today. Ban tam Book, 1970.

7   2 A Clan: A large group of thousands of people who have a common and similar traditions, and who claim common ancestry.

8   Westermann Dietrich. The African To-day. London: Oxford University Press, 1934, p.206.

9   A Runyoro word for education.

Mythologies, legends, genealogies, proverbs, oral history, music, dance, drama, nature of the universe, codes of conduct and speech were inculcated into the young. In some large kingdoms, training in leadership took the form of exposing sons of rulers to court manners. The young pages were thus trained in the arts of service and war. Modes of livelihood among the common class were sometimes inculcated by means of apprenticeship, at the end of which apprentices were initiated into the trade.

> A systematic and intense course of education was imparted in the initiation rites, at the period of transition from childhood to adult life, and of admission to full membership in the group.[10]

By undergoing a series of initiations, young members of a community are brought into the spiritual inheritance of their forebears. Customs and ideals of the society are thereby handed over to posterity by such initiation rites. The rites are considered important for the welfare of the society and its unaltered continuance. The initiated become willing members of the community which includes the ancestors. Hence, the strong sense of community, still a living force in Africa.

Historical Aspects of the Problem

The history of modern education in Uganda starts with Catholic and Protestant Missions, which arrived in the country during the last quarter of the 19th century. Although Islam had been introduced into the country long before Christianity, it had not taken firm roots by the time of the arrival of Christian Missions. The primary motive of Arab Moslems in the country had, hitherto, been trade rather than propagation of Islam. It was the arrival of Christian Missions that threatened the expansion of Islam and created an atmosphere of religious competition that erupted into bloody wars between Moslems and Christians, between Protestants and Catholics, and between the exotic

---

10   Hoernle A. W.., "An Outline of the Native Conception of Education in Africa, "Africa, Vol. IV, pp. 145-63.

religions and the non-committed or animists. The early history of Education in Uganda was enacted by two religious factions, namely Protestant and Catholic Missions. The Moslem faction did not at first show interest in Schools beyond the religious ones which taught the reading of the Koran.

The interest of early Missions extended beyond teaching their converts the art of reading the Bible. Mackay, an early protestant Missionary in Uganda, "taught Africans the rudiments of wood craft and engineering."[11]

Bishop Tucker, the second Protestant Bishop in the country, arrived in 1890. By then there were six schools with a student population of 454.[12] In the following quotation will be seen the aim behind this early education. The Bishop wrote this in 1898: "The course of our story now turns to education, or, as it has been fitly described, character-making. For what after all is education but the moulding of the character in high and noble ideals?"[13]

From this missionary concept of education originated the creation of a new Christian schooled African, so uprooted from his past that he had from thence to be known and called by new biblical names, seek a white collar job in town and imitate indiscriminately his European teacher. The following quotation, which clearly portrays missionary educational activities in Africa, is most apt for Uganda:

> The missionaries have arranged their schools for their own purposes. They have to care for the religious education of Christian children, but at the same time they regard the schools as a means of missionary propaganda, since they are attended also by pagans. For the missionary the interests of his religion or his Church are naturally paramount. This is clearly shown by the character of many of the village mission schools, which often fail to satisfy even the modest claims of a general education. They may even incur the suspicion that they make use of secular knowledge merely as a bait to fill their classrooms, and then show their scholars the way into their Church.

11   Jones, Gresford H. Uganda in Transformation. London: 1926,
12   Ibid., P.117.
13   Ibid., P.117.

Like every other activity of the white man, the school, and especially the school in the hands of the mission, has a destructive effect on social cohesion. The missionary aims at replacing the indigenous religion by a foreign one, and in doing so he strikes at the very root of Native life. Religion is so closely associated with all other departments of life that this destructive effect is inevitable, even when the missionary proceeds with the greatest caution, which is not always the case.

There are two main schools of thought among missionaries about these problems. One school sees Christianity and Western civilization on the same plane. Even if they do not regard them as identical, yet for them they are so closely bound together that the one is not thought of without the other, and the union of the two is expressed in the term 'Christian civilization. The institutions and outlook of the West are the ideal, and to transplant this Christian ideal to Africa is the aim of their work. Where Native institutions are different from our own, they are unchristian. To succeed in replacing African customs by European or American is a victory of the Christian spirit. According to the personal outlook of the missionary he may in his efforts emphasize the Christian or the civilizing side, but in essence both are one.[14]

Christianization and European cultural indoctrination went hand in hand. The success of the former was measured by that of the latter "Ambivalence of the African toward his heritage,"[15] a problem which is plaguing present-day educators in the country, has its root in this early education. To the Mission's way of thinking everything African represented paganism, and an African who had lost his culture was bound to remain a firm Christian.

School subjects bore no relevance to real life of the people. African Music was considered pagan and despised by the teachers and pupils.

While Christian Missions were busy founding schools, the British Colonial Government was preoccupied in building up administrative machinery and establishing law and order. It was soon realized by the Colonial Government that a little schooling would increase the usefulness of the African; and a comprehensive policy making was begun in 1920.

14   Westermann Diedrich. The African Today. London: oxford university Press, 1934, pp. 218-219
15   Hanson, John W. Imagination and Hallucination in African Education. Michigan State University, 1967.

This interest in education was further stimulated by the trustees of the 'Caroline Phelp Stokes Trust' who resolved to send from the U.S.A. a Commission to East Africa to visit Kenya, Uganda, Tanganyika,[16] Basutoland, Swaziland and Ethiopia on 21st November, 1923, in order to study African Education on the spot.

The Commission was led by Dr. Thomas Jesse Jones, a U.S. citizen. It included among its members Dr. Garfield Williams, a British from the Church Missionary Society, and Professor Aggrey, an African from the Gold Coast[17] then teaching in the United States of America.

The significance of this Commission is firstly in the fact that African education had attracted international interest; secondly, largely as a result of the Commission, the British House of Commons appointed a permanent Committee to report to H. M. Government on African Educational Affairs; and thirdly, the significance of the Commission is in what was recommended, expressing their concern for lack of relatedness in the existing system of education: "Education must be enlarged, and better adapted to the needs of the native people."[18]

On 24th November, 1923, the British Secretary of State for the Colonies appointed an 'Advisory Committee on Native Education in the British Tropical African Dependencies'[19] whose terms of reference were to "advise the Secretary of State on any matters of Native Education in the British Colonies and Protectorates in tropical Africa which he may refer to them; and to assist him in advancing the progress of education in those Colonies and Protectorates"[20]

In 1925 the British Government assumed an ever increasing interest in Uganda's Education, as can be seen in the following memorandum which constituted the earliest declared British Government Policy of Education in Uganda:

Government welcomes and will always encourage all voluntary educational effort which conforms to the general policy. Cooperation

16   Now Tanzania
17   Now Ghana
18   Jones, Gresford H. Uganda in Transformation. London (1926), p. 185.
19   British Colonial Office: Education Policy in British Tropical Africa. (British
        Parliament Papers by Command cmd. 2374) London: H.M. Stationery Office, p. 1.
20   Ibid.

between Government and other educational agencies should be provided in every way................................ Education should be adapted to the mentality, aptitudes, occupations, and traditions of various people, conserving as far as possible all sound and healthy elements in the fabric of their social life. Its aim should be to render the individual more efficient in his or her condition of life, whatever it may be, and to promote the advancement of the community as a whole through the improvement of agriculture, the development of Native industries, the improvement of health, the training of the people, in management of their own affairs, and the inculcation of true ideals of citizenship and service.[21]

A policy of partnership in the running of African education was thus formed between Government and Missions. Government financial aid to Mission Schools was unfortunately subjected to examination results although this had not been the original intention, as can be seen in the following quotation:

The policy of encouragement of voluntary effort in education has as its corollary the establishment of a system of grants in aid to schools which conform to the prescribed regulations and attain the necessary standard. Provided that the required standard of educational efficiency is reached, aided schools should be regarded as filling a place in the scheme of education as important as the schools conducted by Government itself. The Utilisation of efficient voluntary agencies economises the revenues available for educational purposes. The Conditions under which grants are given should not be dependent on examination results.[22]

In practice there was no other means by which the Mission's Schools attainment of 'the necessary standard' was arrived at by Government except through studying examination results. School work became examination centred, and education was narrowed down to bookish work.

Examinations were prescribed by Government and some of them prepared in England for British and unrelated to the African students. So education became bookish, and school subjects were divorced from the real life of the African student.

---

21   Jones Gresford H. anda in Transformation. London (1926), p. 125
22   British Colonial Office: Education Policy in British Tropical (British Parlia ment Papers by Command cmd. 2374) London H..M. Stationery Office, p. 7.

Agencies which founded and administered Primary School Education were Missions, and later on, Moslems, Private Individuals and Local Governments. The Agencies financed the schools from tuition fees, private donations and Central Government grants. The Government grants covered the salaries of teachers only. Building construction, maintenance and equipment were financed from tuition fees and private donations.

Largely as a result of this system, we note a disparity in education. Tribal or culture groups most receptive, or having easy access to education benefited considerably to the extent that Post-Independence Government has seen this imbalance in educational development as a cause of disunity. The problem was further aggravated by religious animosity and competition.[23] Protestants and Catholics competed in their process of evangelizing the country to the extent that Schools and Churches were built next door to each other and sometimes away from real centres of population. Consequently, children had to go long distances to obtain education. Where spacing of schools is reasonably fair, some children have to pass the nearest school in search of schools of their own denomination.

In 1952 an attempt was made to create a homogeneous Primary School Administrative body. This was contained in the recommendations of the de Bunsen Committee:

> We regard it as fundamental that within the policies determined by the Protectorate Government, the responsibility for local educational planning of Primary education should rest with the District Local Education Authorities who will, we hope, create their own local development schemes and stimulate through School Boards of Managers a real and increasing sense of local responsibility for the first five years of Education.'[24]

Since 1953 there has been a marked interest in education at all levels in Uganda.

23   See Religious Wars referred to on page 6.
24   Report: African Education in Uganda (1952), p. 1.

It was during the same year that the Price Assistance Fund was renamed African Development Fund (£20,000,000) and resorted to in the general development of education. Of this amount £ 8,000,000 was set aside for educational expansions and innovations. The Fund was used up in six years, having financed Teacher Training Colleges and Secondary Schools, all of which have a direct effect on Primary education.

The problem of Primary School drop-outs is due, among other causes, to uneven distribution of schools which involve children in travelling long distances, to and fro, for their education.

Several classes are run at half capacity of pupils.[25] Normally Primary I and II have maximum number of pupils, but enrollment falls in classes above Primary II.

> In 1951, 66,405 boys were enrolled at the bottom classes of the Primary Schools throughout Uganda. This showed that well over 75% of school age boys attended school in their lives, if only for a term or two. Enrollment fell off rapidly. Only 19,657 were enrolled in Primary IV; 9,080 were enrolled in Primary VI; and 1,831 were enrolled in Junior Secondary III (now the equivalent of Primary VIII).[26]

Consequently, the Committee on "African Education in Uganda" (de Bunsen Committee) of 1952 emphasized the need for consolidation of existing Primary Schools rather than expansion:

"Very broadly speaking, as many children now enter Primary School System as the economic state of the country justifies, and the main aim should be to ensure that those who enter stay on for the fullest course which can be made available to them."[27]

The year 1959 heralded a new government policy of education contained in Uganda Government Session Paper published in February of that year. The Paper dealt with Primary and Secondary education of all races. The problem it considered was one of Consolidation rather than expansion.

---

25   Forty is regarded as maximum number of pupils per class in Uganda.
26   Report: African Education in Uganda Protectorate (1952), p. 13.
27   Ibid.

However desirable expansion might seem to be, for the next few years the principal effort should be directed towards raising the standard of teaching in all grades of Schools and providing a minimum of four years of schooling for all who desire it with the ultimate objective of a basic course of eight years for every child.[28]

At the end of 1960 the number of Government and Grant-aided Primary schools in the whole country was 2,354, with a total enrollment of 346,000 African children (108,000 girls), 16,000 Asians and 1,100 Europeans.'[29]

The majority of schools were managed by Missions (voluntary agencies), a number of schools were run directly by local government, and a few were privately owned.

The year 1961 heralded for the first time in the history of Uganda a pre-independence National Assembly with a majority of African Representatives. The following private motion was introduced into and adopted by the Assembly:[30] "Be it resolved that this House urges Government to introduce the teaching of African music in Uganda Teacher Training Colleges."[31]

1962 was the year of Uganda's independence. One of the first actions of an independent African Government was to appoint Commission under the chairmanship of Professor Castle to study and report on Education. In its report the Commission laid emphasis on Secondary School expansion and reaffirmed an earlier decision to expand the Primary School course to eight years.

One of the most important decisions taken by the Commission was to propose multi—denominational Teacher Training Colleges, and to propose formation of multi-denominational Primary Schools where there was need for some. This is bound to result firstly, in evenly distributed schools; secondly, in decline of religious influenced management of schools; and thirdly, in a balanced secular and religious instruction in Primary schools.

The comprehensive expansion of primary education from six to eight years is

28   Uganda: The Making of a Nation, p. 21.

29   The Making of a Nation, p. 21.

30   The Motion was proposed by the writer of this Dissertation, then a member of Uganda National Assembly.

31   Hansard: Uganda National Assembly Official Report of Parliamentary Debates Entebbe: Government Printers, 1961.

being formed with full speed since 1962. Notwithstanding the implementation of this recommendation, the problem posed by immature Primary School leavers is immense and far from being solved.

The Castle Report did not go far in its reference to need for curriculum changes. It simply stated: "The governing principle in curriculum building is summed up in the word 'relevance' and curriculum should be relevant to the present and future needs of Uganda."[32]

Independent Uganda pledged in 1962 to eradicate "ignorance" in its society.[33] This goal impinges on the function of education in that universal primary schooling has become an educational objective. There has followed a steep rise in Primary School output graphs.[34] The effect on 'educational Pyramid' is that the middle and the upper heights begin to resemble more closely the slopes of a real pyramid, in contrast to their previous resemblance to a narrow spear perched upon a broad, low box.

Owing to limited funds available for educational expansion, Secondary Schools and other Post-Primary institutions cannot absorb all primary school output. These institutions have resorted to a selective system which stamps the rejected as failures:

> The selective system is inclined to worry less about those who leave prematurely because, as we noted, its traditional mission, above the primary level, has been to winnow out the most promising and form them into an educated elite which will guide the affairs of society. Through its screening and rejecting process, it stamps large numbers as failures before they even have the chance to choose for themselves whether they will struggle on or become dropouts. In such circumstances, a 'failure' may be crippled for life.[35]

Many of the "failures" cannot find jobs, so they add to the unemployed. This is aggravated by the fact that during their education they received no vocational

---

32   Report: Uganda Education Commission (1962), p. 27.
33   Policy Statement of the then ruling Political Party: The Uganda Peoples' Congress.
34   Coombs, Phillip H. The World Educational Crises. London: Oxford University Press (1968), p. 66.
35   Coombs, Phillip H. The World Educational Crises. London: Oxford University Press (1968), p. 68.

guidance which can only come through use of carefully conceived curriculum. Young children should be given a chance to prove and develop their personalities to enable them to sufficiently play their part in the drama of life and progress of society.

During the course of their education, unfortunate attitudes are formed. The attitudes formed, very often, make them covet white-collar jobs and disapprove of manual labor and technical vocations. School subjects bearing no relevancy to real social and cultural life of Uganda turn out children who are city oriented. The 'failures' rather than turn to development of their family lands run to the cities to join the unemployed.

Problems Challenging Music Education

Music curriculum must progressively reflect political, social and ethical values of the society. Hence, the need to investigate and establish a genuine philosophy for the education of the young which is regrettably absent in Africa at the present moment.[36]

A music curriculum must focus on society:

> All education proceeds by participation of the individual in the social consciousness of the race. This process begins unconsciously almost at birth, and is continually shaping the individual's powers, saturating his consciousness, forming his habits, training his ideas, and arousing his feelings and emotions.[37]

Promotion of all such worthy cultural features as would contribute to a better future and mature the ideal quality of life in the educand, should be the function of a music curriculum. Corollary to this, is the call to mitigate against the unfortunate 'ambivalence of the schooled African toward his heritage, and to eradicate divisive elements in society which are sustained by unhealthy religious competition and negative ethnocentricity.

Education has been defined as:

---

36   Notable exception being President Julius Nyerere's "Education for Self-Reliance which adopts Socialist educational concepts for Tanzania's education. p. 427.

37   Dewey, John, "On Education." New York: Modern Library, Inc.,

The stimulation of the child's powers by the demands of the social situations in which he finds himself. Through these demands he is stimulated to act as a member of a unity to emerge from his original narrowness of action and feeling, and to conceive himself from the standpoint of the welfare of the group to which he belongs. [38]

Music education must help a child to grow and mature, to put service of mankind above personal gain, to learn how to live successfully with others, to gain skill and knowledge, to develop a respect for high standards and values and to find his own place in society.

A music curriculum must broaden the mind of the educand by promoting appreciation of music of other cultures as well as his own. This will open the way to his acceptance of differences in cultures. "It is an irony of fate that in order to avert a catastrophic World War, 'man' must bend every effort to realizing a truly human society."[39]

All this necessitates a deep sense of commitment on the part of a teacher in order to "guide growth" and to effect a requisite "changed behavior"[40] in the child.

In a developing nation like Uganda, faced with educational poverty and plagued by low enrollments, high wastage rates, gross differences in educational opportunities, and a growing rate of unemployed primary school leavers, it is important that the proposed music curriculum should take note of the country's meager resources without denying general music education to every child.

Philosophical Aspects of the Problem

It has been suggested that African Religion can be depicted as triangle.[41] At the top, head of all powers, is God. On two sides of the triangle are the next greatest powers, gods and ancestors. At the base are lower forces, with which magic and medicine are concerned. Man is in the middle, and must live in harmony with all powers that affect his life, family and work.'[42]

---

38   See Page 8.
39   Dewey, John, "On Education." p. 147
40   Fannie Shaftel R., "Values in a World of Many iltures," Educational Leadership 18 (May 1961), p. 489.
41   Mursell, James H., "Growth Process in Music Education," from "Basic Concepts in Music Education," NSSE (1958).
42   See Figure 1, page 21

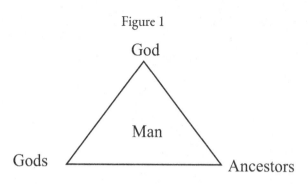

Figure 1

Man's life is dichotomized into birth, infancy, puberty, adult (marriage), death and succession. Each of the dichotomies forms important landmarks in one's life with definite educational experiences in which music plays a leading role.

Figure 2 below is illustrative of life and its dichotomies:

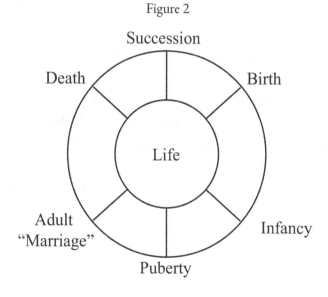

Figure 2

The act of preparing, training and transforming a young child into a mature responsible person was and still is of utmost .importance in a community. A child had to be inducted into the heritage of his predecessors[43] manifested in the music, poetry, art, drama, dance and stories including mythologies, legends, genealogies, proverbs and oral history of the country.

Figure 3

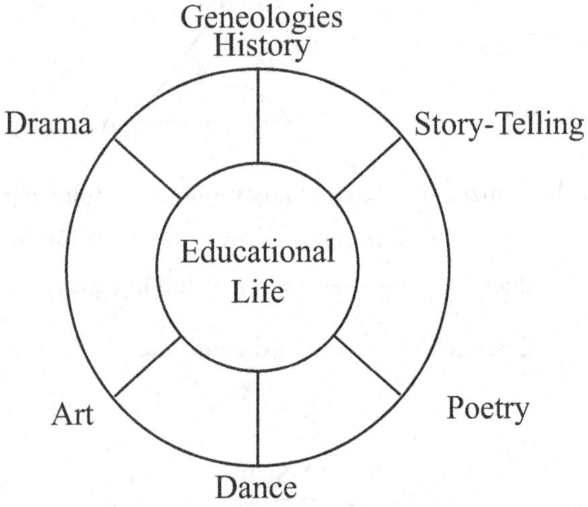

Geneologies
History

Drama

Story-Telling

Educational
Life

Art

Poetry

Dance

The life-cycle of an agricultural community as represented in Figure 4 below revolves around production of crops. Weather and 'Mother Earth' play their part in such production. They are forces that are unpredictable. However, they are assured to the community if man lives in harmony with all powers that affect his life namely, God, the gods, and ancestors. Man is therefore obliged to fulfill all rituals pertaining to the agricultural activities indicated in Figure 4.

---

43   See Figure 3

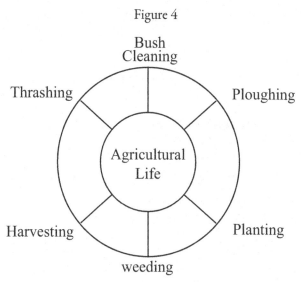

Figure 4

Schools have come into existence in Africa because civilization has grown complex, so the formal method of education has been superimposed upon the traditional or informal method, unfortunately without prior study and appreciation of the latter. Such ill-conceived formal education has produced members who no longer conceive themselves from the standpoint of the communities which they are expected to serve and offer effective leadership.

2

Justification

Philosophical Basis for Teaching Music

Music plays a unique role in the life of the African; it provides a medium between the living and the dead. Through Music, invocation of ancestral spirits is achieved. Similarly, communication between man and his gods is provided through the medium of Music. The spiritual role of Music is illustrated in Figure 5 below:

Figure 5

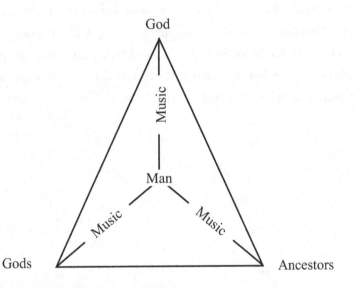

Each of the dichotomies indicated in Figure 2 is characterized by its own music. There is music for birth, for infancy, for marriage, for adults and for death.

In the ritualization and dramatization of each of the life's dichotomy, music plays the main role as is indicated in Figure 6 below:

Figure 6

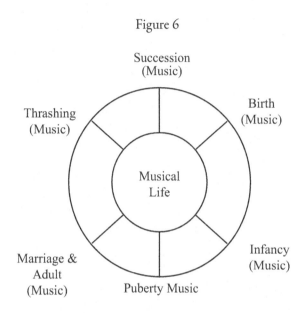

Music is indispensable for all man's feelings and emotions. It expresses his happiness and jubilations at wedding and festivals, his pride and sophistication at court, his loneliness and devotion at religious rituals, his simplicity and humbleness at home by his fireplace and his bravery and courage at war.

Music is used by verbal artists to accompany oral history, storytelling, speech making and various forms of poetic recitations. Genealogies, proverbs, legends and mythologies are all portrayed through music. In fact, music is the most effective medium through which children are inducted into the heritage of their ancestors.[44]

Schools have come into Africa because civilization has grown complex, so the formal method of education has been super-imposed upon the traditional or informal method, unfortunately without prior study and appreciation of the

---

44   See figure 7

latter. Such ill- conceived formal education has produced members who no longer conceive themselves from the standpoint of the communities which they are expected to serve and offer effective leadership

Figure 7

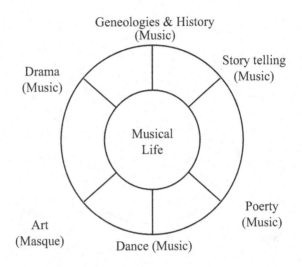

Life means growth, and living has its own intrinsic quality which becomes the main concern of education. Each of the dichotomies of life referred to in Figure 2 has that quality, and should, therefore, interest educators.

It is essential that the African be educated by his social environment. He will thus become a sharer or partner in the activities of the society; its success will become his success and its failures his failures. It is only through this means that he will become a servant and a leader of his people.

> When nature and society can live in the classroom, when the forms and tools of learning are subordinated to the substance of experience, then shall there be an opportunity for this identification, and culture shall be the password.[45]

---

45   Dewey, John. The School and Society. The University of Chicago S, 1943

Contribution of Music Education to National and Cultural Building

Uganda is still plagued by negative ethnocentricity which beset proper growth and development of a young nation. A rich music curriculum which draws on all diverse cultural heritage could contribute effectively toward production of mature individuals who would actively contribute to national and cultural building:

> The individual who is to be educated is a social individual, and that society is an organic union of individuals. If we eliminate the social factor from the child, we are left with an abstraction; if we eliminate the individual factor from society, we are left with an inert and lifeless mass ..... [46]

Most unfortunate is the fact that modern ill-conceived education has produced a large number of "inert and lifeless mass," who are uprooted from their society, and no longer act as members of a unity, or conceive themselves from the standpoint the group to which they belong. Not only are the educational products "inert and lifeless," but they are extremely disunited and incapable of offering effective service and leadership to their communities.

Need for Relevance in Music Education

Music pervades all African social environments.[47] It is the medium through which the African expresses all his feelings and emotion. Therefore, in music all arts, drama, poetry, dance, oral history and folklore have been conceived and bequeathed to posterity.

---

46   Archambaut, , Reginald D. (Editor) John Dewy on Education. Library, p. 429.

47   See figure 8

Figure 8

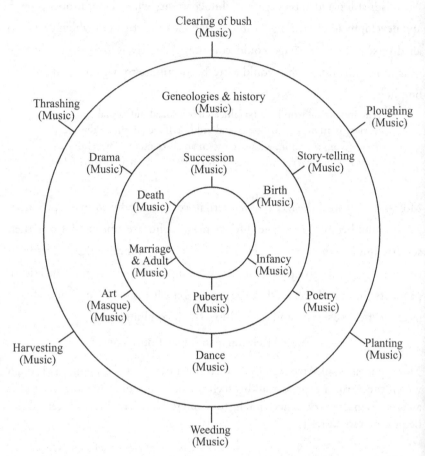

This enhances the importance of African Music in the school curricula. Failure to relate school music to real life and experience would and has created loss of value in and disrespect of African heritage among Schooled Africans. Devaluation of African culture and general ambivalence toward African heritage may create psychological repercussions in the educand. Education should not separate a child from its environment.

> Education has two sides, one psychological and one sociological. The psychological and sociological sides of the child are organically related. The child's own instincts and powers furnish the material

and give the starting point for all education, but knowledge of social conditions, of the present state of civilization, is necessary in order to properly interpret the child's powers. The child has his own instincts and tendencies, but we do not know what these mean until we can translate them in their social equivalent.[48]

The loss is not only spiritual but it is also technical. Exclusion of African Music from the school curricula has led to formation of generations of men and women who are incapable of performing music. The skills of performance and the rules of the art are gradually disappearing.

Traditionally, music plays a most predominant role in the culture of Africa.[49] If schools are to be the spearheads for promoting, encouraging, and stimulating a continued evolution in the culture of Africa, they must enhance growth and continued influence African Music to function as a true element of that culture.[50]

Inculcation of High Standards and Values in Life

Positive experience in early childhood tends to create confidence and bring forth morally positive reactions. Through an interrupted series of favorable stimuli of conscious and sub-conscious character, an ego is being formed which will allow for a natural formation of moral super ego, and the result will be a mature and well directed personality.[51]

Exclusion of African Music from the mission—conceived school curriculum was and still is tantamount to contempt of the natural joys of young people, and a worst form of oppression and suppression of man's happiness. It is indicative of lack of psychological interest in, as well as absence of "love" for the educands. This absence of "love" strikes a sharp contrast to the principles of Christian teaching: "Suffer the little children to come unto me."[52]

---

48   Dewey, John. On Education. Modern Library, p. 428. fer to Figure 8.
49   Refer to Figure 8
50   Mbabi-Katana, S. Preface to Introduction to East African Music Adult Education Centre, Agip House, 9 Kampala • BOX 7176, Kampala, Uganda.
51   Ulrich Robert. History of ucational Thought. New York1 Van strand Reinhold Co. (1968). /On Pestalozzi, p. 261./
52   Jesus, quoted in St. Mark 10:14.

Love is a pre-requisite to good teaching. It was John Gerson, a medieval educator, who postulated: "Love is the Source and end of education.[53]

A child centred curriculum is a result of considerable interest in, love for and understanding of children. It is intended to provide much more than mere cultural conditioning. "If knowledge and study cannot transcend conditioning, then probably nothing can, and music education can be only one more species of conditioning.[54]

Music education should lead to progressive development and deepening appreciation of the art. Music should ultimately become a great instructive influence in the life of the educand.

Appreciation of Music of the World's Cultures

> The deepest source of development and education lies in the experience of love which a person has as a child in relation to his parents. If a child is put on this 'road of nature' he will understand without many words the most essential moral elements of human life, namely, fellowship, peace, gratitude, and justice.[55]

According to Pestalozzi,

> The sphere of knowledge from which man in his individual station can receive happiness begins closely around his own self and his nearest relationship; from there his knowledge will expand, and while expanding it must regulate itself according to this firm centre of all powers of truth.......... Educate only in this 'path of nature,' then men can understand and estimate one another because they will develop a pure sense of simplicity and uprighteousness.[56]

This offers support to the African concept of education which has its foundation in the family, and which gradually expands the horizon of a child from family to broader relationships.

---

53   Ulrich Robert. History of Educational Thought. New York: Van d Reinhold Co. (1968), p. 100.
54   Nelson, Henry B. (Editor) Basic Concepts in Music Education. Chicago: NSSE, p. 83.
55   Ibid.
56   Ibid

Education should liberate children from prejudices and lead them to discover great ideas and to aim at love, respect of life, an appreciation of the dignity and greatness in the Worlds Art. As Friedrich Froebel points out: "Education should lead the child to relate his experiences organically one with another. Thus the child will realize his own personal unity and the unity inherent in diversity of life."[57]

Development of Creativity

"Childhood is not merely a preparation for adulthood, it is a value in itself and possesses its own creativeness"[58] Life and its dichotomies are illustrated in Figure 2 on page 16. Each dichotomy constitutes highly valuable experiences ingrained with qualities and values most interesting to educators who seek to reconstruct such experiences for enrichment of the minds of the educands and stimulation of their powers of creativity.

The purpose of learning should not be mere continuance of tradition; it should aim far beyond this goal in order to assist the educand toward a higher degree of self-expression, and a better understanding which leads to independence of thought and spontaneity of action in the field of creativity. The ultimate goal being growth and enrichment of art and full enjoyment of life.

A music curriculum must aim at exposure of children to the best there is in music and performance. Through life itself children must so broaden in knowledge and skill that ultimately music has to become a powerful constructive force in their lives.

---

57   Ulich, Robert. History of Educational Thought. NewYork: Van Nostrand Reinhold Co. (1968), p.288.
58   Quotation of Johan Heinrich Pestalozzi in: Ulich, Robert. History of Educational Thought. New York: Van Nostrand Reinhold Co. (1968), p. 258.

3

Method

General Music Education

General Music is required of all pupils in Grade 1-7. Music belongs to all, and the task of a music teacher constitutes the act of "bringing music and people closer together." [59]

General Music experiences will spring from the still living folk heritage illustrated in Figure 8 on page 23. The following words of Kodaly meant for Hungarian Folk Music, equally apply to Uganda Folk Musical heritage:

> Folk music is not primitive music, but an art that has matured in an evolutionary process lasting a thousand years ……. So far it is the most consummate musical expression of our national spirit……[60]

Those simplified and worthy elements of the African environment[61] which are deemed capable of contributing to a better future for our children will be committed to symbols and be ingrained into the daily activity of the school.

Over one hundred and fifty songs of various degrees of difficulty and involving various activities, have been drawn from the traditional East African Musical heritage, and committed to symbols.

The school will thus be made to absorb in successive stages graded musical heritage, which has been committed to symbols and made available to all children irrespective of their social limitations.

It is hoped that elimination of two kinds of musical illiteracy will be achieved through teaching people, on one hand, to read music, and on the other hand, to appreciate true musical values.

---

59   Eosze, Laszlo. Zoltan Kodaly: His Life and Work. London: Collet's Holdings, Ltd. (1962), p. 39.
60   Ibid., p. 83
61   Illustrated in Figure 8 on page 27.

Alongside the 150 songs, there will be graded sight reading and memory exercises in tunes and rhythms. Musical growth will be stressed at every level and in every activity.

> Musical growth depends altogether upon study of and dealing with music itself and upon differentiating the constituents which determine its significant expressiveness, its beauty. Musical growth does not depend upon studying those constituents in isolation.... It becomes evident once again that the all-too-common distinction between the musical and the technical is a fallacy. Rhythmic organization, key relationships, phrase structure, and so on, might be thought of as technical considerations, and in a sense they are. But at the same time they are the constituents upon which the whole effect of music and the art of music itself depend. They must be progressively apprehended or musical growth itself........ becomes impossible.[62]

The curriculum will progressively provide for discovery of aptitudes, and differentiation in needs, interests and abilities, and will accordingly strive to cater for such specialties and introduce use of flexible programs.

Integration of Various Related Learning Experience

In a Uganda Primary school, the usual practice is to have one teacher offer instructions in all subjects in his class. Because of such self contained class rooms, a trend toward the core curriculum integrating various related learning experience is being emphasized. In this way, a highly divided curriculum that separates artificially the "segments of life common to all people"[63] will be avoided.

---

62   Quotation from Mursell, James H., "Growth Proces is Music Education," p. 150, in Nelson, Henry B.(Editor) Growth Process in Music Education. Chi cago, NSSE (1958).
63   Douglass, Harl R. Principles and Procedures of Curriculum Improvement. The Douglas Series in Education.

Thus the following related learning experiences, all of which are integral parts of the Folk heritage[64] will be incorporated into a Music Class: Poetry, Drama, Story-telling, Art (Masque), Crafts (making of musical and stage instruments), Dance and Physical Education games.

It is thereby hoped that additional time gained will automatically benefit all subjects. "Time is to a school subject what water and sunlight are to a plant"[65]

Use of Para-Professionals

Owing to the country's meager financial resources, there are limited funds available for education.[66] It is the general class teacher, rather than music specialist, that is envisaged in this curriculum.

However, there is expressed in the curriculum, need for employment by each Primary School, of a demonstrator-artist obtained locally and cheaply on either part-time or full-time basis, who would assist in instrumental training and participate in concert production.[67]

Through such para-professional artists, it is hoped, a wealth of traditional African verbal artists' knowledge will be portrayed in a living form to the Music class. Music, Poetry, Story-telling, Proverbs, Folklore in general, and Dance will thus be made available to school children.

It should be emphasized, however, the entire responsibility of teaching a music class would still rest with the general class teacher. The para-professional artist's role would be that of assisting the general class teacher, by filling in his expertise knowledge where it is required in the normal lesson, and by displaying his art at concerts and some other production

---

64   See the illustration in Figure 8 on page 27.

65   Broady, K.O., "Enriched Curriculum for Small Schools," The Small School in Action Series.

66   Refer to page 16.

67   The practice of hiring, on part-time basis, of local artists exists in some schools in Uganda. It is proposed here that the system be officially confirmed and widely practiced throughout the country.

Flexible Scheduling

The curriculum, in order to cater for individual pupils, recommends that differentiation should be progressively achieved by: ability grouping (special sections), homogeneous grouping (interest groupings, electives), diagnosis and remedial treatment, extracurricular activities, and individualized learning.

Consequently, it will be necessary to introduce a system of flexible scheduling as indicated below, bearing in mind that the maximum number of pupils per class is 40, and that the time allocated to general music class is 150 minutes per week, or a minimum average of 30 minutes daily.

Primary Grades One and Two -Under the supervision of two classroom teachers with the assistance of a local demonstration artist.

On **Mondays, Tuesdays,** and **Thursdays**, the classes will be taught by their teachers – playing, writing and reading of simple rhythms, rote singing, listening, dancing, learning poetry, singing play songs as well as story songs, and acting.

On **Wednesdays** and **Fridays** – classes will be combined (see Figure 9) and the time will be devoted to performance by pupils of materials learned in class. On some occasions local executant artists will be invited to perform to the classes.

Teachers will seize this opportunity to observe and evaluate their pupils regarding general development and behavior change with respect to sense of responsibility, co-operation, gaining of skills and knowledge.

Figure 9

Class scheduling for level I

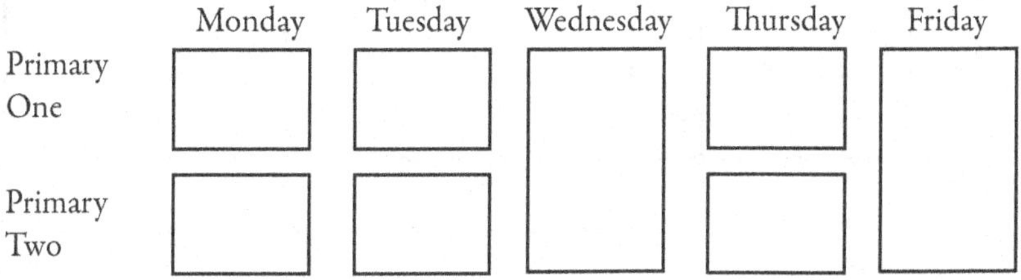

	Monday	Tuesday	Wednesday	Thursday	Friday
Primary One					
Primary Two					

Primary Grades Three, Four and Five – Under the supervision of four teachers, including the demonstrator-local artist.

On **Mondays, Tuesdays,** and **Thursdays**, the combined three classes will be divided into four groups: A large group of 75 pupils and three small groups of 15 pupils.

> Pupils in the large group will be offered self-administering individualized material.
>
> Selection in the small groups will be based on ability, electives and diagnosis or remedial treatment.
>
> It is in the small groups that the services of the demonstrator (local artist) will be needed for studies on musical instruments.
>
> Instruction offered to the small groups will include playing, writing and reading rhythms and tunes, listening, singing songs, reciting poetry and story songs[68] singing of play songs, acting, and learning the craft of making instruments.

Wednesdays and **Fridays** will be devoted to concerts, etc.

Figure 10

Class Scheduling for level II

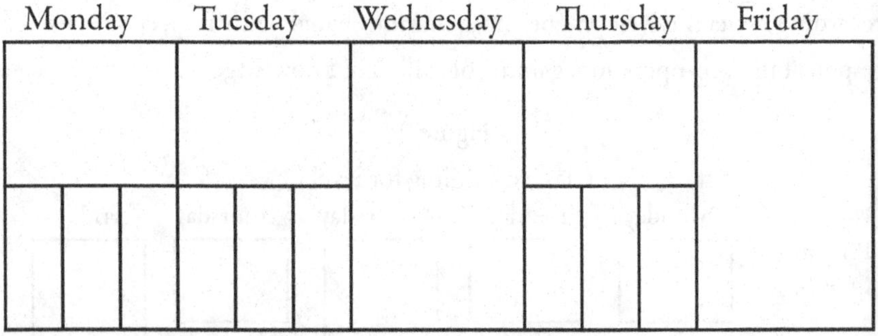

Monday	Tuesday	Wednesday	Thursday	Friday

---

68   Recitation of poetry and storytelling is more often declaimed or chanted, to ac companiment of a musical instrument, than spoken.

Primary Grades Six and Seven – During each of the first four days of the week (Mondays to Thursdays) the combined three classes will be divided into the following groups:

A large group of 90 pupils and three small groups of 10 pupils per group.

Pupils in the large group will be offered individualized materials which are self-administering. It is hoped the pupils will be motivated and directed at every step by the material itself.

Pupils in the small group, based on either ability, or electives, or diagnosis and remedial treatment, will be given instruction in playing, writing, and reading rhythms and tunes; listening, dancing, singing, poetry, play songs and stories, acting, performance skills, and making instruments.

Fridays will be devoted to performance by pupils of materials learnt in class, while teacher will utilize this opportunity to observe and evaluate musical growth and artistic maturity of each pupil.

On some occasions, executant artists, local or otherwise, will be invited to perform to students.

Figure 11

Class Scheduling for level III

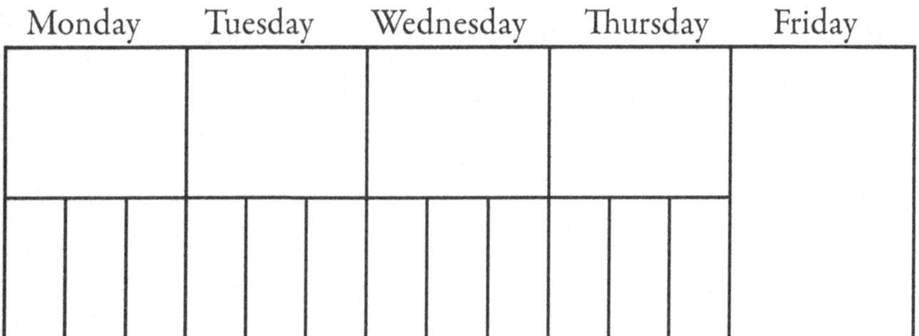

Monday	Tuesday	Wednesday	Thursday	Friday

General Music in Primary School–Learning will generally take the form of reduction of tension in relation to solving problems involving wholes.[69] Growth and development will thus be reflected in the order of topics which should always reappear in new setting with added meaning.

Alongside this progressive development will be a careful ascertainment of pupil's interest, channeling it along suitable lines of action while at the same time pursuing integrated development.

Continual evaluation will be necessary in order to ascertain pupil's level of maturation, which should determine his position in ability grouping and the level of individualized material on the one hand, and distribution of work load in the program of study and practice.

Efforts will be repeatedly made to clearly demonstrate to the pupil goals and objectives, so as to enable him to discern requisite standards.

In conclusion, it should be emphasized that owing to Uganda's limited resources, it will not be possible to use film-strips and to employ music specialists at Primary schools for many years to come. However, it will be possible to cheaply utilize the services of local executant or verbal artists of high caliber at school concerts, during practice hours in class, to demonstrate new techniques, correct faulty techniques and inspire and motivate pupils to acquiring further performance skills.

---

69   Nelson, Henry B. (Editor), "Basic Concepts in Music Education." NSSE (1958)

4

Review of Related Literature

None of the books reviewed in this chapter contributes to the data of this dissertation. The purpose of writing this chapter is to demonstrate the inadequacy of available literature on Uganda music, as well as convey general information on studies that have so far been carried out on the subject previous to the writing of this dissertation.

A number of early European travelers and missionaries left useful information on Uganda. They covered a wide field of studies embracing political, social, economic and physical aspects of the country.

Their information on Uganda music, however, is sketchy and tale-like. On the whole it seems to have been prompted by curiosity and replete with ideological or cultural bias.

> In 1945, the Trustees of Uganda Museum, probably through the influence of Dr. K.P. Wachmann,[70] expressed in their annual report, interest in the future of folk music in Uganda.

> Presumably, that annual report was instrumental in prompting the British Colonial Development and Welfare Fund to sponsor in 1948 a "Regional Collection of Folk Music under Scheme R. 233."[71]

The scheme was conducted by Dr. K.P, Wachsmann, who had already been making investigations on Uganda folk music on his own. His "Folk Musicians in Uganda" is based on the 'Research Scheme R. 233,' as is his contribution to a book entitled 'Tribal Crafts of Uganda," published in conjunction with Margaret Trowell, M.B.E.

---

70   Dr. K.P. Wachsmann was the Uganda Museum curator at the time.
71   Wachsmann, K.P. Folk Musicians in Uganda Kampala: The Uganda Museum, 1956.

First Systematic Approach to Uganda Music – For the first time a systematic approach to the study of Uganda music is noticeable as a result of Dr. Wachsmann's publication. In spite of his scientific methods, he attached great importance to judgements of folk musicians as can be read in the following admission: "Working with folk musicians has taught an important lesson, namely, to allow their attitude towards music to guide the student."[72]

He makes a careful appraisal of the bias of the minds of listeners to and performers of Uganda Folk Music. From this standpoint he makes interesting descriptions and evaluation of the music, as well as an attempt to dispel misinformed judgement on the music by non-Africans.

He makes interesting assumptions on the history of the country, arrived at through speculating on rhythmic and melodic characteristics of Uganda Folk Music; and notes a strong social impact created by a broad song spectrum observable in Uganda Folk Music. He also raises interesting issues relative to the usual formal pattern of Uganda songs, which gives rise to a characteristic responsorial style of singing.

On the whole, the book serves one important purpose, namely, it raises interesting and highly intriguing points which merit further investigation. Most significant are the following two remarks: "Uganda might claim not only geographically but musically, a place between West Africa and the Orient,"[73] and "Of course, the music of Africa with all the diversity of its peoples and their histories, can no more be uniform in concept than the music of the 25 Uganda tribes can be reduced to a common formula.[74]

---

72   Wachsmann, K.P. Folk Musicians in Uganda Kampala: The Uganda
        Museum, 1956, p. 2.
73   Wachsmann, K.P. Folk Musicians in Uganda. Kampala: The Uganda
        Museum, 1956, P. 1.
74   Ibid.

An Anthology of Uganda Musical Instruments – Dr. Wachmann's precise classification, description and anthology of African (Uganda) sound instruments forms a monumental work in the study of African music.[75]

His classification of the instruments is based on E.M. von Hornbostel.[76] He divides sound instruments into the following four groups: Idiophones, Aerophones, Membrophones and Chordophones.

Dr. Wachsmann's ethnological account and descriptions bearing on the instruments was the first of its kind. The originality of this work enhances its value.

The work is purely ethnological rather than musicological or both. However, the omission of music in no way reflects on the significance of this work to musicologists. In fact, a subject as vast as Uganda Sound Instruments could not have been better tackled.

The work as a whole is precise and basic in nature; hence, its referential value for ethnographers, historians, musicologists and educators.

The First Transcription of Uganda Xylophone Music – Notwithstanding the fact that only one tribal xylophone music is covered in **African Music from the Source of the Nile**, by Joseph Kyagambiddwa,[77] the work merits a review in this dissertation mainly because it forms one of the first attempts to transcribe Uganda Xylophone music into conventional notation.

Regrettable, however, is the fact that the xylophone scores are unintelligible even to someone who understands the Ganda xylophone patterns. Similarly, a good many historical statements made in this book have not been substantiated.

---

75   Wachsmann, K.P. The Sound Instruments (Part Two of Tribal
        Crafts of Uganda. Margaret Trowell and K.P. Wachsmann), Oxford
        University Press, 1953.
76   Hornbostel's classification of sound instruments as shown in Africa,
        Volume VI, p. 303
77   Kyagambiddwa, Joseph, African Music from the Source of the Nile.
        New York: Frederick A. Pareger, 1955.

However, the publication of sixty-two xylophone scores is a major step in the study of Uganda music.

The First Theory Book on East African Music – In 1961, a 'Research and Training in African Music' program was launched by the author of this dissertation through the financial assistance of a Rockefeller Foundation Grant to the University of East Africa, with the aim of training and developing musically talented teachers in teaching techniques.

An Introduction to East African Music for Schools, by S. Mbabi-Katana,[78]

is a sequel to an extensive collection of 150 East African songs which form the main data of teaching materials appearing in this dissertation.

In **An Introduction to East African Music for Schools**, the author demonstrates clearly the meaning and use of the musical elements of notations, pitch, time, intervals, scales, and rhythm with special reference to the indigenous music of East Africa.

The book was written with the aim of providing East African teachers and students with a background knowledge of musical elements based upon examples drawn from their national songs. It was also the hope of the author that the publication would enhance a true understanding of the national songs and growth of African Music to function as a true element of the cultures of the new developing nations of East Africa.

---

78   Mbabi-Katana, S. An Introduction to East African Music for Schools. Kampala: Uganda Adult Education Foundation, 1966.

5

Exposition of Data

This chapter deals with the exposition of the main data for this dissertation, which consists of 150 songs. In the next chapter, reference will be made regarding additional data, which are in the form of phonograph records, musical instruments, various poems, plays and dances.

The main data consists of 150 folksongs. Their inclusion in the dissertation as Course Work is intended to ensure their availability to readers.

The songs were collected and transcribed under a scheme entitled: "Research and Training in African Music," conducted by the author and financed by a Rockefeller Foundation Grant, for the purpose, to the University of East Africa.

The songs were drawn from a rich and vast folk heritage of the East African Nations of Kenya, Uganda and Tanzania, and from some related ethnic groups to be found in neighboring countries of the Republic of Congo, Rwanda, Malawi and Burundi.

The East African folksong is consummate, rich and varied. It is mature, and some of it has weathered centuries of evolution. It portrays immortal musical achievements of past generations, as well as bears witness to otherwise forgotten centuries of African life.

As a product of the rustic population, the folksong is simple and sincere. It appeals to all people and justly claims the epithet of National Art. Indeed, it forms the most consummate musical expression of the national spirit of the countries of East Africa

Figure 8, on page 23, illustrate the predominant part played by folk music in the African social environment. The rich variety and multiplicity of functions of the songs in the Course work confirm, further, the important role of music in the African social environment. Hence, the significance of songs in explanations of various phenomena of African life.[79]

It should further be stressed that a collection of national folksongs, such as one appearing in the Course Work, portrays "man's cumulative behavior"[80] or culture. Consequently, the understanding of the songs and of the rich and varied folklore they contain would enable one to achieve an organic cultural growth in an ever-changing Africa, and to develop a quest for the deeper meanings in not only the Art of Music, but also in the nature of man himself. In this way music should be looked at as a great instructive influence in the life of students.[81]

As a chief receptacle of man's 'cumulative behavior,' folk music reveals multidimensional aspects of man's life. From the standpoint of man's movement in time, folk music manifests the past, present and gives direction to the future of man's achievements. From the standpoint of man's movement in space, folk music conveys a picture of man's conquests, migrations and expansion in space. From the standpoint of man's existence in society, mention has already been made of the predominant part played by folk music in the African's social environment.

Interesting Sidelines Studies

The songs appearing in this dissertation represent a wide variety of African folk music and broad social spectrums. In this dissertation they serve a limited function of building up 'a music curriculum for the first seven years of schooling.' The author's comments are, therefore, restricted to this task and to making additional notes as would facilitate the teaching of the songs.

79   Regrettably, the significance of folk music in the African Studies has, so far, only been dimly realized.
80   Merriam, Alap P. Prologue to the Study of the African Arts. 1961.
81   Refer to last paragraph under subtitle "Inculcation of High Standards and Values in Life" on page 29.

Nevertheless, it should be pointed out that, in the long run, a collection of songs, representing a wide variety of African folk music and cultural heritages such as one appearing in the Course Work, is bound to contribute considerably to understanding of related aspects of learning and to aid in answers to such questions as the following:

Could similarities of musical phenomena over several and scattered areas in Africa be used as indicators of geographical origins of present ethnic groups, or of historical expansions, migrations and conquests, and of the history of man's conquest of space in Africa?

Could a collection of songs such as the one appearing in this dissertation aid in the study of African cultures and their interactions, in view of the fact of folk music being interdependent upon dance and language, should it not hold a key position in the study of cultures?

Could African music be used to identify presence or otherwise of African musical traits in the music of the Afro-Americans, to determine the extent or rate of musical changes, and to answer questions such as to what extent does change of language play in accelerating such musical changes?

Could the songs in the Course Work with their various musical styles and startling variety of musical idioms be reduced to certain basic principles of sound construction and be used to provide a basis for testing the universality of such principles in the music of the world regardless of cultural contexts?

A Musical Perception of the Words of the Songs

The three main language groups of East Africa, namely, Bantu, Luo and Nile-Hamitic, are represented in the songs appearing in this dissertation.

A general and brief study of the musical accents in the words of these languages is most significant because, generally, it is the word that gives rise to a tune in most of the songs quoted in the dissertation.

In several instances, melodies are so totally word-conceived to the extent that it is the word that determines the timbre or voice quality, pitch or location of the voice in a tonal scale and rhythm including the dynamic and durational aspects of the notes of melodies.

Consequently, a general musical perception of the words of the song is considered essential and necessary to facilitate the teaching of the songs.

Timbre – Is conceived here as the quality of tone and pronunciation of both consonants and vowels as conditioned by the shape of sound passages, namely, mouth, nose and throat.

All the languages referred to above are written in Roman alphabets which, as a result of long usage, have become established as pictures of all the word sounds. Consequently, alphabets are used below in illustrating the timbre characteristics of the language.

A good practice in the correct pronunciation of the following common consonants will facilitate the reading of the words of the songs:

Timbre Characteristics	Consonants			
Bilabial	p	b		
Bilabial nasal	m	mw		
Labio	w			
Labio dental	f	v		
Alveolar	t	d	n	
Sibilant	z	s		
Palatal	c	j	y	sh
Velar	g	k		
Velar nasal	ŋ			
Guttural	h			
Lateral trill	r	rr		
Glotal	a! (For stopping or refusing it implies a warning)			
Pre-nasalised bilabial	mp	mb		

Pre-nasalised labio dental	nf	nv	
Pre-nasalised alveolar	nt	nd	nn
Pre-nasalised sibilant	nz	ns	
Pre-nasalised palatal	nc	nj	ny
Pre-nasalised velar	ng	nk	

The following table will illustrate the timbre characteristics of common vowels found in the words of the songs:

	Lip Spread	Lip Rounded	
Mouth closed and front	i	u	Mouth closed but back
Mouth half open and front	e	o	Mouth half open and back
Mouth open	a	/////	

Pitch – The rising and falling of voice is an inalienable element of speech in all the language represented in the songs appearing in this dissertation. Every syllable in a word has a special pitch relative to other syllables.

In consequence of different pitches of syllables between themselves, every word gets a certain intonation whose movement is either level when all syllables have the same pitch, falling when the pitch of the ultima is lower than the pitch of the root syllable.

The intonation of the words can become combined in view of different derivations and position in a sentence. The intonation may be raised or lowered according to the elevations of the tone, which is not only determined by the meaning of the word, the sentence, or sentence group, but also by the feeling of the speaker.

Generally, three pitches are discernible (High – Middle – Low) and are graphically represented here below:

Example 1

High _____

Middle _____

Low _____

In a majority of songs in this book, there is a duality, in a varying degree, between the gradation of the pitch of spoken words of a song and that of the tune of a song. Song number 30 quoted here below is designed to illustrate the duality between speech tones and the music of the song:

Example 2

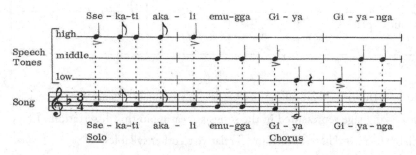

Lying at extreme ends are examples of songs in which the duality does not exist at all. At one extreme are those songs whose tunes are word-conceived; and at the other extreme are tunes which are purely melismatic, such as the one below taken from song number 76:

Example 3

Rhythm – Is conceived here as embracing the dynamic and quantitative properties of sound. Rhythmic accent manifests itself in two dimensions: dynamic and quantitative. Dynamic accent is in turn perceived in three gradations: the strong, half-strong and weak accents.

A strong accent may fall either on the root syllable of a word, or on the penult, or on the ultima. Similarly, a half-strong or weak accent may fall on either syllable.

A strong accent which is heard as the strongest in a word may fall on different syllable of the word. Similarly, both half-strong and weak accents may fall on different syllable of a word.

Quantitative access is the duration aspect of rhythmic stress. It manifests itself in vowels, consonants and syllables. A vowel or consonant or syllable having any of the dynamic accents may be long or short in a strict proportion of 2 to 1.[82] That is to say, if the time unit for the long accent is one, the time unit for the short accent is half.

In ordinary communications of ideas or opinions, a speaker produces sounds whose qualitative accents have fixed time values that can be expressed in notation in which degree of dynamic accent is realized.[83] The notation represents measured rhythm with strong accents occurring anywhere as in prose. This type of notation could be played on a membraneous drum or idiophonic slit-drum. The sounds thus produced could convey a message to listeners a long distance away.[84]

When words are arranged as they are in a song, with regular alteration of strong and weak syllables, they assume a close relationship with music which also has various schemes of accented and unaccented notes.

Poetry is based on such patterns of regular alternation of strong and weak accents. Poetry improvisation with instrumental accompaniment is a cherished

82   See Example 2
83   See Example 2.
84   A verbal message is also communicated on a talking-drum which is
      technically equipped to express both the rhythmic and pitch accents in a word

art among the cultures whose songs are quoted in this dissertation. Poetry improvisation is developed a stage further and married to music. Hence, the remarkably close relationship between speech and singing in the various languages whose songs are quoted in the dissertation.

Word-conceived rhythmic stress, both durational and accentual, is a regular phenomenon in the songs quoted in the dissertation. Therefore, primacy of text is an indisputable factor for a successful and accurate rendition of the songs. Clarity of pronunciation and correct accentuation are indispensable for a successful execution of the songs.

Form in the Songs

A fusion of text and tone giving rise to a dual art is a feature that has already been observed in the songs in the dissertation. It is the text that shapes a melody tonally and rhythmically, imparts color to it, and makes a song what it is.

> Composers and interpreters alike approach the song through the poem. They study its structure, the movement of the verse, the organization of its lines, rhyme and stanzas. These are important, for the poem gives form to the music.[85]

In determining design in the songs appearing in this dissertation, due attention is being focused on the poetic forms of the texts of the song

Strophic form is common for most songs in the dissertation, basic characteristic pattern of which is that the same music is repeated for succeeding stanzas. Within this framework there are numerous variations.

In a number of songs we note the strophic repetition is resorted to only to break the pattern of monotony in the course of the song. The form here is referred to as Modified Strophic.

---

85   Hall, James Husst. The Art Song. Norman: The University of Oklahoma Press, 1953, p. 4.

There are a few examples of songs in which there is no musical repetition, and the entire song is through-composed.

So, we have three clear types of song forms observable in the Course Work. It is these three forms that merit a detailed discussion in the pages that will follow.

Strophic Form – Whose common feature is that all stanzas of the text are sung to the same music. The design is not limited to simple lyrics, it is frequently met with in dramatic and narrative texts as well. It is in the latter type of texts that music, owing to its being word-conceived, in its formal structure follows closely that of the text.[86]

Within the strophic song form there are subtle variations brought about by a typical two-part structure of melodic style known as responsorial, in which the first part is sung by solo and the second part by a chorus. It is the subtle interplay between solo and chorus that creates the variations to the plain strophic pattern. In the succeeding discussion these variations will be given alphabetical groupings.

Group A – consists of plain strophic form in which the same music is repeated for every stanza in a poem. In this group there is no responsorial pattern. The song in this form may be sung by one individual or by a group of singers. For precise examples of this form, the reader can look up the songs whose extracts are indicated below:

Example 4

Song Number 99

Twi – ri–rwe tu – go–nye Mn_____ Twi – ri–rwe tu – go –

---

86   This point has been exhaustively discussed under "A Musical Perception of the Words of the Songs," p. 49.

Example 5

Song Number 88

Uũũ   ki - ra

Group B – in which each stanza has a refrain, a stanza is given a complete musical idea, and the same idea is repeated to the words of the refrain. The reader is advised to refer to the songs whose extracts are indicated below:

Example 6

Song Number 85

Nga - ya - ya   nga - ya - ya Mu - hu-ma wa - nge

Example 7

Song Number 127

Ku - mi - tu   ku - ta - le   va - ka - ndo   le -

Group C – whose features are: the solo part is an incomplete music idea and its complementary part is the chorus. A good example of this design is found in the following songs:

Example 8

Song Number 44

Ki-so-ma bwi - re itu - mbi ka - lya - tu - mba Ki - so-ma

bwi - re ota - li - nso - me - ra omwa - na

Example 9

Song Number 30

Sse - ka-ti aka - li emu-gga Gi - ya Gi - ya - nga

Group D – in which the solo's part is long while the chorus is short, often consisting of one word as in the following example:

Example 10

Song Number 68

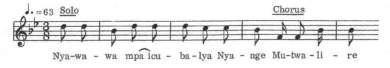

Nya-wa - wa mpa icu - ba-lya Nya - nge Mu-twa - li - re

Group E – is one in which the chorus part is interpolated, here and there, in the music. Structurally, there is no clear-cut musical division of the part for solo and chorus, for example:

Example 11

Song Number 81

Ki - na-tsi Ki - le-ngu-ru-ma Ki - na-tsi___ Ki - le-ngu-ru-ma

Group F – is one in which there is a partial super imposition of the solo and chorus parts. This is due to entrance of the solo before the end of the chorus part. The result is two-part music. A good example of this form can be found in the following:

Example 12

Song Number 146

nsa - nze aba-lu - ngi ba - na - nge

Ba -yi - nda nko-le-ntya nsa - nze aba-lu - ngi ba - na - nge

Group G – in which there is complete super imposition of the solo and chorus parts resulting in part music, in which the chorus sings on an ostinato like part while the solo part is free. The following example is the simplest available:

Example 13

Song Number 106

Group H – in which the solo and chorus may be or may not be superimposed upon each other, but a distinct feature of the group is in the chorus section being sung in several parts. The parts may range from 3 to 8. The following example is typical:

Example 14

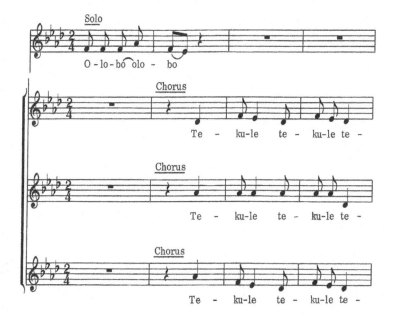

Modified Strophic Form – In this form repetition is resorted to as a unifying factor at some moment in the course of the song. Apart from such repetitions, the song is through-composed.

For a good example of this design, the reader's attention is drawn to song number 144, extract of which is given below:

Example 15

Hoy mo-mo ke-re-bet   Hoy mo-mo ke-re-bet   Ki - be-ndi ma-ra-

This opening section of the song recurs again and again in the course of the song.

Through-Composed Song Form – In which music matches the poetry, so much so, that at times unifying continuity in the music seems absent.

However, this is the most advanced art form in which music aims at capturing the meaning of each phrase and illuminating each word.

A simple example of this form is found in song number 104, an extract of which is quoted below:

Example 16

Ki - ku - ru   Sha - ri - sha
Ri - sha   She - nde - kwi

Conclusion

In conclusion, the author wishes to stress the musical significance of a spoken word in the African musical art as has been pointed out earlier on in this chapter; he also wishes to suggest, in this connection, new and important sideline studies.

The vastness and complexity of the subject of musical significance of spoken words rules out its discussion in this work. It merits a separate dissertation. However, it is necessary to emphasize one musical aspect of the spoken words, namely, rhythm, and draw out its potentials as a sideline study.

Earlier on in this chapter observations were made regarding the nature of word rhythmic patterns and their arrangement in songs and drum messages. It is from these observations that the author wishes to advance in simple terms a new concept of the nature and foundation of African rhythms. A majority of songs in the Course Work bear witness to the fact that their rhythmic patterns are text-derived. Therefore, a concept of "verbal foundation of African rhythms" if fully investigated is bound to supersede earlier concepts on the subject of African rhythms.[87]

---

87   In 1928 Dr. Eric von Hornbostel propounded the concept of "Motor Foundation of African Rhythms." (E.M. von Hornbostel, 1928-"African Negro Music." Africa, Vol. 1, No. 1.)

6

Treatment of Data

The data for this dissertation will be classified and reduced to learning experiences suitable for the age and maturity of students. The classified data will be structured in a logical form in which they can be easily presented to students.

There are several methods of presentation, but the most common one which is frequently recommended in the sample lesson-plans appearing in the Course Work is rote method.

The following is a general description of rote method of presenting a new song: Firstly, a teacher pronounces the song text and explains its meaning to class. Secondly, he pronounces the words of the text as the class repeats them after him. Thirdly, as fluency in pronunciation of the words is gained, the teacher sings the song through, drawing attention of the class to any point of importance in the music. Fourthly he sings the song phrase by phrase as the class sings after him. This process is repeated in longer passages until the song is mastered as a whole.

Classification of Data

Classification has as its aim simplification and clarification of material to be classified. Classification must be simple, easy and assimilable. A classification that does not achieve this aim is bound to remain a meaningless and illogical exercise.

The present classification is motivated by a desire for classification of the main data for this dissertation. The classification has been made broad in order to produce clarified and assimilable classifications. The data has been cast into four functional categories, namely, story songs, play songs, dance songs and general songs. The value of this broad and comprehensive division is enhanced by the fact that multiplicity of functions typical of African songs is reduced to a simple assimilable form.

Each of the four classifications has been recast into three broad subdivisions based on degree of difficulty of the songs. The three subdivisions correspond with three levels of musical maturity.

The first level of musical maturity encompassing Primary Grades I and II correspond with the first subdivision. The second subdivision is designed for the second level of musical maturity involving Primary Grade III, IV. The third sub-division constitutes course work equivalent to the third level of musical maturity attributable to Primary Grades V and VII.

Broad levels of musical maturity encompassing two or three school classes do not create any educational hazard, in fact, based as they are on flexible scheduling, they do offer an opportunity to teachers for putting into practice skilled planning and inventiveness in instructional methods. The broad levels of musical maturity provide an operational field in which there would be discovery of aptitudes and differentiation in needs, interests and abilities, as well as application of the following schemes: ability grouping (special sections), homogeneous grouping (interest grouping, electives), diagnosis and remedial treatment, extracurricular activities and individualized learning.

Purpose of function of a song, and its musical and textural structures are determinant factors of the degree of difficulty in the song. A song with a simple purpose does not require long and elaborate music or text, a factor that explains the facility with which present classification has been achieved.

It has already been established that there are musical traditions surrounding childhood life with a wealth of songs, dances and musical games of all kinds.[88] Musical traditions are dichotomized.[89]

---

88   See Chapter II, second paragraph on page 23.
89   See Figure 6 on page 24.

This dichotomy has naturally facilitated the present classification and the musical experiences contained in each classification have been drawn from it. The African musical traditions are highly reliable in their age group dichotomies; needless to say, such dichotomies have been established by custom and experience.

From what has been pointed out in previous chapters, it is apparent that African music is not a luxury but a part of the process of living itself. Before the advent of modern schooling, children whose ages range from 6 to 9 years were left to themselves to engage in their own pastime activities which had values in themselves and possessed their own creativeness. It is from such activities, namely, musical plays, songs, dances and stories that the learning experiences for the first level of musical maturity have been drawn.

Within the age group ranging from 9 to 12 years, children could begin to discharge simple duties under constant supervision of their elders or parents. Their way of life was changing as they approached puberty.[90] This change is marked in their past time activities from which learning experiences for the second level of musical maturity have been drawn.

The age range of 12 to 16 years formed a group of boys and girls that were about to or had already had puberty initiations. Before the advent of modern schooling, this age group discharged adult duties for their parents. Girls would prepare meals in aid of their mothers and do various domestic duties. Boys would do men's work such as looking after cattle or felling trees, clearing bushes or participate in hunting expeditions. Their adulthood experiences climaxed in marriages, at which stage they assumed full adult responsibilities.

This age group corresponds with level III of musical maturity in the envisaged curriculum for the Primary School Grades V, VI and VII.

---

90   Last paragraph on page 5 refers to intense and systematic traditional education of this age group.

Treatment of the Classified Contents

Essentially, it is the same learning experiences that are to be progressively provided at all levels of musical maturity with the aim of bringing about evolution of musical responsiveness. And the learning process which is conceived is that of gradually clarifying understanding.[91]

Such progressive development would, hopefully, lead to achievement of great depth in appreciation of the art and would bring about conditions in which music would become a great instructive influence in the lives of students.

It is the progressive grasp of musical concepts which is held as the main instructional objects that coincides with the long term behavioral objectives envisaged in the dissertation, namely, attainment of a condition in which music would become a great instructive influence in the life of a student.

With this objective in mind, the instructional objectives outlined in this book are structured in the following fundamental and logical manner:-

Figure 12

Integrated Aspects of Music Study

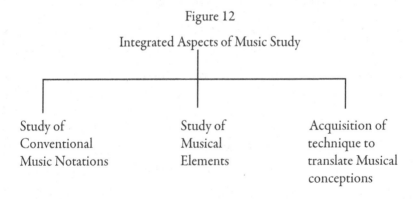

| Study of Conventional Music Notations | Study of Musical Elements | Acquisition of technique to translate Musical conceptions |

The above structure emphasizes study of integrated learning experiences, and learning by wholes of materials adopted to the age and maturity of children;

---

91   Refer to quotation on page 33 taken from James L. Mursell, Growth Process in Music Education

the fundamental condition for learning must be an element of familiarity, along with introduction of new factors which produce problems. The arrangement would be in a "Cyclical Sequence."

> ... the various items that need to be presented do not occur once for all at some predetermined time, they appear again and again, always in new settings, always with added meaning.[92]

Progressive introduction of conventional musical notations which, in actual fact, symbolically represent music concepts right at the beginning to the first level of music maturity.

> Even the vague and incomplete understanding which is all one should contemplate in the early years is impossible if all symbolism is excluded on some ill-judged principle.[93]

Right at the beginning of the first level of musical maturity there should be a progressive introduction of the elements of music which ultimately make up the content of music theory. At first, they should be introduced vaguely, but as time goes on and experience and maturity gained by the students, the full significance of the elements and their interrelatedness will emerge.

One has to bear in mind that music is a tonal art and its theoretical knowledge is best developed from music itself, hence, the significance of listening experience. Listening experience is a controlling factor in pursuance of the music program conceived in this dissertation. This point will be developed later on.

This program is chosen for its suitability to the age and maturity of students guided by an important concept, namely, music forms part of a natural setting in which students play and work together as is evidenced in the sample-lessons appearing in the Course Work. All the time teachers will have to bear in mind the following important precepts"

---

92   Nelson, Henry B.(Editor). Basic Concepts in Music Education. NSSE (1958), p. 157.
93   Ibid.

... it is the musical content of the program that determines the presentation of musical concepts. Music is chosen for its own intrinsic worth, not for the sake of illustrating or teaching the so-called fundamentals. And the concepts for dealing with it are developed as occasion suggests.[94]

Materials for Instructional Use during Listening Experiences

Musical concepts are factors that engage the attention of the listener. All integrated aspect of music study utilize listening experience. Conventional notations which represent symbolically musical concepts must be heard in order to be understood. Similarly, a proper grasp of technique to translate musical concepts hinges upon good listening experiences and ability to pre-recognize aurally the concepts.

Consequently, the value of a listening experience which is completely integrated in the overall learning experiences cannot be overestimated. Listening experience is highly contributive to both the short term instructional objectives and the long term behavioral objectives already referred to in this dissertation.

It is suggested in the lesson-plans appearing in the Coursework that before a song is sung by students they should hear it as a whole sung by their teacher. The method of teaching suggested would enable them to learn the song as a whole or by phrase, and their singing will be an expression of what they have heard.

From such simple experiences, listening habits will be formed that would aid students in listening to recording that have been made by professional artists.

Listening experiences along with other learning experiences should be properly guided and focused upon progressive development of musical understanding. Available phonograph records entail upon a teacher the task of grading of and selecting from a wide range of musical styles in Africa. However, the last of

---

94   Ibid.

the following records has been specifically designed for educational purposes by the author. Hugh Tracey's Music of Africa Series, UNESCO "Ocora" Series (supplied with anthologies in French and English), Folkways: The World Ethnic Music (supplied with anthologies in English), and Mbabi-Katana's Music of East Africa for Schools (available at the Institute of Education Library, Makerere University, Kampala, Uganda).

One of the aims pursued in the building of this curriculum is that children should be liberated from prejudices and encouraged to discover greatness in other cultures. It is in the listening experiences that this important task will find expression.

In order to satisfy this important need the following phonograph records are suggested for listening experiences: instruments of the Orchestra (22 full Orchestra pictures, J. W. Pepper and sons), Great Masters' Repertoire of Children's Music, Carl Orff's Music for Children (two records, 33 1/3), and Andrelle Manning's original children's activity songs (33 1/3).

Treatment of Musical Instruments

Instruments upon which progressive acquisition of technique should be developed are human voices, drums, xylophones, marimbas, bamboo flutes, Sansa (thumb pianos), rattles, wood blocks, bells, sets of side-blown trumpets, lyres, harps, zithers, bow lutes[95] and recorders.

Traditionally, technical skills in playing or singing music had been handed from one generation to another until the advent of modern schooling which disrupted the traditional educational means and failed to absorb them into its system. The result musically was loss of technique.[96] There followed generations of men and women who were and are incapable of performing music.

95   For description of the instruments, the erader is referred to Trowell and Wachsmann. Tribal Crafts of Uganda. London: Oxford University Press (1953).

96   The loss is also spiritual, as is discussed on page 18 under "problems challenging music education."

Throughout this work, especially throughout the sample lessons appearing in the course work, music is conceived as a natural part of a setting in which students will learn to work and play together so as to rightfully derive maximum joy and pleasure from the art. It is conceived that music-making will pervade the entire setting for music education.

Acquisition of technique to translate musical concepts is part and parcel of the integrated aspects of musical studies already referred to in this chapter, and achievement of this technique is a logical result of a well-conceived music curriculum.

Treatment of Dance

Dance with its attendant rhythm and music plays a great part in the life of the Africans. For the African, music and dance are not separable, nor are they a luxury, but part of the whole process of living.

Music tradition surrounding birth of a child, which begins before the birth of baby at the seeking of a diviner's message regarding safe delivery of the baby, consists of music and dance.

Musical and Dance ceremonize birth of a baby, especially of twins. Infancy and childhood life is a welter of songs, dances and musical games.

Puberty is a momentous occasion marked by circumcision, music and dance. Singing and dancing mark marriage ceremonies, also death and funerals. Succession ceremonies are joyful occasions marked by contemplative songs and dignified dances.

Singing and dancing form a medium through which benevolence of the spirits is sought before some project is undertaken. Similarly, singing and dancing are used in seeking protection against the inclement elements, at the new moon, at various seasons and sundry agricultural festivals.

The spells and prayers of medicine men are accompanied by singing and dancing. They do often produce healing.

In this dissertation no attempt will be made to refer to sociological or psychological aspects of dance. It is technique that is our concern, as is seen in some sample lesson-plans appearing in the course work.

It is sufficient to mention that two types of dances, namely, ordinary social dance and ceremonial dance, have been introduced. They are all communal in nature and are accompanied by drumming, singing and rhythm-making.

Most of the dances have an underlying idea which pervades the entire performance. For example, in a war dance, dance movements follow the patterns of fighting, the songs speak of war and praise bravery, and the mood of the whole show is martial.

Modes of occupation are also reflected in dance patterns. For example, most of the songs of pastoral people are normally in praise of cattle, in particular bulls, and the dance patterns are imitative of movements of cattle.

It is important for a teacher on introducing a song or dance to a class to be familiar with any underlying idea there might be in the song or dance.

Treatment of various related learning experiences

Earlier in the dissertation mention was made of need for a core curriculum integrating various related learning experiences. The reader will notice that story-telling, poetry, drama and physical education have also been incorporated into some of the sample lesson-plans appearing in the course work.

Art in the form of masques is an integral part of the African ritual dances. Significantly, it symbolizes the underlying idea of a dance and it is a teacher's task to exploit the functional role of the masque so as to benefit his or her teaching of art.

The presence of drama, poetry, stories, proverbs and riddles in the African folk song is indisputable. The 150 folk songs which are the main data for this dissertation form a rich mine of African oral traditions upon which it is hoped a teacher could draw, not only for enrichment of his music lessons, but also for benefiting other subjects.

In the main data there are numerous examples of story songs, ballads, funeral dirges, epics and sundry praise songs. Needless to mention, several narrative and dramatic songs which demand staging and dramatization. Such instances would provide students with full experience through which they may derive enrichment and attain a high degree of self-expression and spontaneity of action in creativity.

Additional data for inclusion in the teaching program may be obtained from a number of books, notably from the Uganda journals (publications of the Uganda Society, Kampala, Uganda).It is also hoped that the already recommended use of para-professional artists would bring to schools the rich local talents of the African verbal artist and thus enrich the program with live performances as well as impart skills to students.

7

Summary, Conclusions and Implications

As has already been pointed out in previous chapters, conceived in this curriculum are three levels of musical maturity. The first level of musical maturity constitutes learning experiences designed for Primary Grades I and II. The second level of musical maturity includes a two-year course of study for Primary Grades III and IV. The third level of musical maturity also is a three-year course of study designed for Primary Grades V ,VI and VII.

Presentation of learning experiences, adapted to the age and maturity of pupils and conceived in an integrated form, will vary directly with the progressive change in musical maturity of students.

The learning of experiences which are presented in an integrated form will be by wholes, notwithstanding the dichotomized experiences in this chapter where the main purpose is to present to the reader fully and in a formative manner, various aspects of the learning experiences.

Should the reader refer to Book I in the Course Work, he will note that the methods suggested in the sample lessons project music as a natural setting in which students work and play together. A song will be presented to the students by the suggested methods, where appropriate musical elements and symbols of notation will be demonstrated aurally and visually. The song will be introduced for its own sake, not for the sake of illustrating elements. The same learning experiences introduced to students at Level I will be progressively pursued with greater depth and added meanings in the study of the succeeding songs for Levels II and III. Thus singing experience will be providing a major medium through which students will be progressively acquiring technique to translate musical conceptions.

The instructional objectives, namely, study of conventional musical notations, study of musical elements, and acquisition of technique to translate music conceptions which are illustrated in figure 12, will be pursued under the following learning experiences: singing experience, rhythmic experience, listening experience, reading experience and composition.[97]

Level I for Primary Grades I and II

Singing experience-The reader should refer to Book I in the course work. There he will find play songs, story songs and dance songs numbering over fifty. They are all in unison, in simple time, and are short and within the age and maturity of the students.

It is hoped that all the songs together with their respective activities will be presented to students. The activity might be dancing, playing or acting. They are all drawn from, and related to the pupils' own childhood environment as illustrated in Figure 2.

The songs will be taught by rote method, and in the course of teaching every attempt will be made to study the song texts, identify underlying ideas and capture the spirit of the songs and activities.

Rhythmic experience-Most of the songs provided for Level I have exciting rhythmic accompaniments such as drumming or hand-clapping or stamping of feet. It is hoped that teachers will exploit such rhythms from the singing experiences. It is also hoped that the musical beats in a song which are clapped by pupils will be written in symbols of notation on blackboard and that the pupils will be allowed an opportunity to copy them.

After a class has learnt to sing a song, they could be divided into two groups. Group I would sing the song, Group II would accompany Group I with

---

[97]   Inherent in these experiences is the concept of Comprehensive Musi cianship, developed in the U.S.A. by the Contemporary Music Project, which acknowledges performing, composing, analyzing and communi cating as constituting a well-integrated music education.

clapping, and a teacher would play on a drum the rhythmic pattern of the words of the song.

As the teacher pronounces the words of the song text and the pupils repeat them after him, as is indicated in the sample lessons he should ask the class to play the patterns on drums or benches. The teacher could, further, illustrate certain drum messages which make use of the same principle, and ask the class to play the messages on drums, or any idiophonic or chordophone instrument and on any wind instrument by playing one note only. Students should be asked to make their own rhythmic patterns and play them.

Listening experiences - Listening experiences will be completely integrated in the overall learning experiences. The rote method of teaching a song, which has already been described in this work, utilizes listening experience. A song is heard as a whole sung by a teacher before the students learn to sing it; and their knowledge of the song is an expression of what they have heard.

Also, listening experience is provided in the following manner: a teacher sings a story song or ballad accompanied by a trough-zither;[98] or the song is rendered by a local professional artist, while the class participate in the chorus part. The class is, later on, asked to relate the story.

Further listening experiences could be achieved through investigations of the simple formal structure of a song. A teacher uses the Solo-Chorus pattern (A-B) of the already referred to story song to illustrate similar pattern in other songs. Later on he could ask the class to identify the pattern in the songs which they have already learnt.

A local artist should be asked to perform music or recite poetry to a class, and students should be encouraged to learn the skill during individualized instructions.

---

98   For a description of a trough-zither the reader is referred to Trowel and Wachsmann. Tribal Crafts of Uganda. London (1953), Oxford University Press.

Reading Experiences – In conjunction with rhythmic, listening and singing experiences it is proposed that musical symbols should be presented on the blackboard. Although at this level the symbols will be vaguely and incompletely understood, it is hoped that as time goes on, experience and maturity will be gained and the symbols will be progressively mastered.

From Book I in the Course Work, a teacher should select songs with undivided beats and scale wise melodic progressions, and use passages from these for reading. Similarly, sight singing exercises should be melodically short and scalewise and should use undivided beat notes.

Composition – It was suggested under 'Rhythmic Experience' that students should be asked to make their own rhythmic patterns and play them; and this is composition. A teacher should endeavor to provide for his students creative experiences and thus integrate composition in the overall learning experiences.

Level II for Primary Grades III and IV

Singing Experience – Book II in the Course Work has over fifty songs, demanding various activities such as acting, dancing and playing. Some of the songs are in compound time, have unusual rhythmic complexities and are in two parts. However, they are all within the age and maturity of the students.

A teacher should plan to teach all the songs together with their activities. He should be familiar with the pronunciation of the words of a song before he introduces it to the class and should take note of the underlying idea there might be in the song and its activity.

The song should be presented by the rote method; but later on, the teacher could distribute to the class a written version of the song so that the class could learn to sing with the aid of written notes.

Rhythmic Experience – Rhythmic experiences for this level should be drawn from the songs being learnt. Many of the songs have rhythmic accompaniments such as hand-clapping, drumming and stamping of feet.

A teacher should write on the blackboard the beats clapped, as well as the rhythmic patterns of the tune being studied, and teach the class to play and sing the written symbols. He should divide the class into three groups. Group I should sing the song, Group II should accompany with hand clapping, and Group III should play the rhythmic pattern of the tune on drums or idiophonic substances or chordophonic or wind instruments, playing only one note. Students should be encouraged to make and play their own rhythms and tunes.

A teacher should introduce to the class some drum messages and some well-known drum accompaniments to songs.[99] Whatever he presents aurally he should write on the blackboard and ask the class to play it and to copy it in their notebooks.

Listening Experience – In addition to listening to story songs as indicated under Level I, a teacher should introduce short instrumental pieces. With the aid of a local artist, a teacher should illustrate different parts of xylophone music, after which the combined xylophone parts could be performed. Similarly, in connection with an instrumental ensemble, a teacher should illustrate the different instruments as well as the theme used before playing the music to his class.

A teacher should develop the two-part formal structure of Solo-Chorus (A-B) referred to under Level I, and make his class aware of contrasts and similarities in music leading to A-B-A formal design. He should ask the class to identify the A-B-A structure in any of the music known to them.

A local artist should be asked to perform music or recite poetry to a class. Students should be encouraged to learn the skill from the artist, especially during individual or group instruction periods.

---

99   Some Uganda drum-rhythms can be found in Mbabi-Katana, S. Intro
       duction to East African Music for Schools. Uganda Adult Education
       Foundation (1967), pp. 52 and 53.

Reading Experience – It is being emphasized that whatever sounds are presented to a class aurally should also be written on the blackboard, and the class should be encouraged to copy the written sounds in their notebooks.

The melodically short and scalewise sight singing exercises referred to under Level I should be continued, but some of the beat notes should be divided into halves. A teacher could introduce very simple tunes for memory exercise.

Composition – In addition to the suggestion made under 'Rhythmic Experiences' that students should be encouraged to make and to play their own rhythms, it is proposed that in conjunction with 'Listening Experience,' students could be asked to supply a chorus (B) to a given solo (A) in a two-part formal structure (Solo-Chorus: A-B).

Level III for Primary Grades V, VI and VII

Singing Experience – A teacher should plan to teach all the songs in Book III appearing in the Course Work. Some of the songs demand certain activities such as acting, dancing and playing. Some songs are long and do abound in intricate expressions. Some are multipart and multirhythmic to such an extent that their rendition requires conducting. Nevertheless, they all fall within the age and maturity conceived for Level III.

Ample time should be devoted to pronouncing the song texts and studying the rhythmic patterns of the words of the texts. The approach would ensure a quick and successful mastery of the songs.

Presentation of a new song by rote method should be resorted to as an aid to reading. Students should by now be able to follow on a song score music as sung by their teacher.

A teacher should be aware of an underlying idea in a song and its activity, and should encourage his students to investigate such ideas in music.

Rhythmic Experience – As has previously been mentioned, rhythmic experiences should be drawn from a song being studied, and rhythmic accompaniments to the songs as well as rhythmic patterns of the words of the song text should be experienced aurally, visually and actively by a class. The class should be familiar with rhythmic notation.

Students should be encouraged to make their own rhythmic patterns and corresponding tunes, and to perform them as well as other known drum rhythms, drum messages, and rhythms taken from some well known music.

A local artist should be asked to perform, to the class, some clan beats, drum messages, or chief's official drum beats. At this stage some students specializing in drumming should also perform to the class.

Listening Experience – In addition to listening experience outlined under Level I and II, a teacher should introduce short pieces of the Music of the World.[100] He should illustrate similarities with and differences from the national music with respect to forms, scales, instrumental and vocal colors, and general expression.

At this stage, a class could start following music on the score, and should be able to indicate on the score a general form of music that is being played. Alternatively, a class could be supplied copies of music scores without expression marks, and would be expected to indicate on the same score appropriate expression marks as they listen to the music.

A local artist should be asked to play to the class live music; also, individual members of the class should perform music for the class on their respective instruments, or recite poems to the accompaniment of a trough-zither or drum.

Reading Experience – Supplementary to the reading encountered in connection with previous experiences referred to under Level III, a teacher should introduce

---

100   The reader should refer to Chapter VI under "Material to Instructural Use During Listening Experience."

to the class appropriate sight singing exercises.

The exercises should be short in length, and generally progressing by step, but a few familiar intervals such as minor third and octaves should be introduced.[101]

Rhythmically, the beat-note used in the exercises should be subdivided into quarters, and rests could be progressively introduced.

Simpler exercises than the ones implied above should be provided for memory training.

Composition – As was suggested under 'Rhythmic Experience,' students should be encouraged to make their own rhythmic patterns and corresponding tunes. They should be encouraged to write and play their own drum messages.

In connection with formal analysis of tunes appearing under 'Listening Experience,' students should be asked to compose their own tunes and to make a formal analysis of their composition.

---

101   Minor thirds are inherent in the five-note scale found in a majority of the songs suggested in the building of this curriculum.

Conclusion

Music plays an important part in the life of the African. It is not a luxury but part of the whole process of living. Before the arrival of Europeans in Uganda, music held a leading role in the traditional African education which has been defined in this work as the act of preparing, training and transforming a young person into a mature, responsible person. The basic philosophy behind this education centred on socialization and maturation of children, and their induction into the accumulated heritage of their ancestors.[102]

Music, itself being a major source of accumulated heritage of the African, it, therefore, needs no justification in the present day general education curriculum. Unfortunately, this is not the case. School education as introduced into Uganda was not based on organic African concepts. Hence, the ambivalence of the modern schooled African toward this heritage, his inability to offer effective service and leadership to his community, and his inability to conceive himself from the standpoint of the group to which he belongs. Disunity and ethnocentricity beset the progress of not only Uganda but most of the young nations of Africa.

Conceived in this dissertation is a child centered curriculum in music based on genuine African philosophy, embodying cultural richness and diversity, and reflecting political, social and ethical values of the society of Uganda. The curriculum is intended to revolutionize music education in the country as well as in the neighboring states of East Africa.[103]

As successful implementation of the curriculum would depend entirely upon teachers' abilities and convictions, it is pertinent to describe in this work conceptions of a right teacher.

---

102   Refer to Figure 3
103   The reader will notice that the songs in the Course Work have been
       collected from all over East Africa.

A teacher should possess an active mind, he should be upright and should practice moderation and proportion in dealing with others, and should be courageous in upholding his convictions. In general, he should be a cultivated man.

> The cultivated man is humane, treating other people with kindness and compassion; and he is sensitive to their feelings, rights, desires, ideals, and attitudes. He is easily approachable, being friendly and hospitable. His humanity extends beyond individuals to social groups; so he may be said to have social sympathies, the habit of referring in thought all pertinent matters to social values and aims, and of emphasizing large social meanings instead of narrow and personally utilitarian. He is also deeply concerned for the improvement of society.[104]

To this must be added progressive knowledge of the nature of the child, knowledge of the subject matter, and ability in discovering and making use of techniques for learner stimulation. All enumerated form the essential characteristic attributes of a teacher.

Knowledge of the child should rank highest among the teacher's needs. Development pattern of one child differs from another. So, for a successful implementation of the curriculum conceived in this dissertation, it is important that the teacher should always endeavor to discover the needs, the capacities, interests, and habit patterns of his student. It is only through this means that the cooperative process of teaching and learning may be adapted to individual needs, interests and potentialities.

The curriculum has been based upon worthwhile goals, it includes learning situations that emphasize individual differences and child activity, and creates learning situations that have relationship to the child's life. In order for the teacher to provide opportunity for the child to solve problems within the limits

---

104   Briggs, Thomas H. Pragmatism and Pedagogy (1940). New York: The Macmillan Company, p. 106.

of his interests and capacities he must discover how each child can benefit from his instruction. He must ascertain the child's capacity for acquiring knowledge and developing right attitudes, emotional and social.

The teacher must evolve a system for evaluating knowledge acquired, skill mastered, and attitudes developed. The results of his investigation must be estimated in terms of the goals set up.

Currently, Uganda schools evaluate acquired knowledge only. However, the objective for evaluation proposed in this curriculum, without disregarding measurement of knowledge acquired, is to help the student to use knowledge in developing positive attitudes and behaviors.

> Genuine test of development is found in what a student does with his capacities in reorganizing himself in light of the particular course; how he meets the responsibilities of the course; the contribution he makes to it; how the course has altered his attitudes; what use he makes of the knowledge acquired.[105]

The evaluation process that is proposed in this work would take into account what the student writes, speaks and does from the beginning to the conclusion of the course. The teacher is expected to determine progress in the development of the student from this information. He should also judge the range of ability and achievement of all members of his class in relation to the educational goals set up which are summed up in the following statement:

> Music should become a great instructive influence in the life of the educand. It should enable him to grow and develop in appreciation and enrichment of the art, and attainment of full enjoyment of life.[106]

---

105   Cantor, Nathaniel. Dynamics of Learning (1950). Buffalo: Forster and Stewart, p. 247.
106   Refer to Chapter II under "Inculcation of High Standards and values in Life."

Implications

Reference has been made to the need for integrating various related learning experiences. Sample lessons appearing in the Course Work treat not only the subject of Music but also Poetry, Drama, Story-telling, Dance, Physical Education, Art and Crafts, all of which are integral parts of the folk heritage. Each of the above subjects has been incorporated into a music lesson as occasion suggests and whenever there has appeared relevancy for it in the music lesson. On the other hand, the entire collection of African folk songs appearing in the Course Work presents enormous opportunities for the study of each of the already referred to subjects, as well as other studies to be mentioned later on.

African Music is an interdisciplinary subject. This fact is increasingly gaining recognition, and many leading musical anthropologists, ethnomusicologists and organologists or scholars of musical instruments are specializing in the study of African Music. Africa has for a long time practiced musical therapy and African spiritualists employ music in the quest of their art.

Music in Africa forms part of the whole process of living.[107] The traditions surrounding man's life stages such as birth, infancy, puberty, adulthood, death and succession are conveyed in Music. Consequently, music is the chief receptacle of man's cumulative behavior, and the chief medium of expression for the African verbal artist.

Poetry – The concept of music and poetry has long been a subject for speculation by scholars and musicians. Aristotle, in his 'Poetics', set forth melody, rhythm and language as elements of poetry. The idea of music as essentially one with the spoken word appears in Wagner's theory about Music Drama. Various contemporary composers of European or Western music have in one way or another endeavored to search for perfect union of words and music. The concept of music as essentially one with the spoken word in African songs has

---

107   This point is well illustrated in Figure 8.

been discussed earlier in this work.[108] The unity between melody, rhythm and language is clearly illustrated in Example 2. So the African folk musician is at the same time the poet.

The importance of the collection of songs in the Course work is further enhanced by their poetic value. The songs do present in their own right a rich source of African poetry, covering a wide range of topics and forming a deep mine of beautiful, philosophical, humorous and highly poetic expressions.

Language – A close relationship that exists between music and speech has been illustrated in Example 2. Such a relationship would point to the possibility of using music in the study of language.

Since musical elements of pitch and rhythm have been shown to be more or less synonymous with those of pronunciation.[109]

The songs appearing in the Course Work are representative of many of the major languages of Africa. There are songs in dialects from Bantu, Luo and Nile-Hamitic languages. Represented in these songs are some of the dialects' best poems, ballads, epics, and stories of all kinds. They are the most authentic examples, and, as far as the author is aware, the first of their kind to be published in such a graded form adapted to school education.

Drama – The folk songs appearing in the Course Work encompass a wide range of social spectrum and cultural heritages. They do offer enormous opportunities for dramatization. In a number of sample lessons suggestions have been made regarding dramatization of a number of songs, especially story songs.

The flexible scheduling that forms the basis of the time allocation in this curriculum, provides for a combination of two or more classes into a single unit on certain days of the week during which there would be performance by pupils and staging of materials learnt during class time.

---

108   Refer to Chapter V under "A Musical Perception of the Words of the Songs."

109   The reader should refer to Example 2.

Art and Crafts – It has already been pointed out that during a musical performance attention is paid to the portrayal of an underlying idea which should pervade the entire show. For example, in a war dance, the dance movements follow the patterns of fighting, and the songs speak of war and praise bravery. Such performances are heightened by the use of appropriate art and crafts. Dancers may paint themselves like warriors with certain designs that have meaning, or they may wear masks that have designs of particular significance and may carry certain implements appropriate for the occasion. It is proposed that such equipment should be prepared by students themselves.

It has already been pointed out in this work that modes of occupation are reflected in dance patterns, that songs of pastoral people are in praise of their cattle, and the dance patterns are imitative of movements of cattle.

The occupation modes are similarly reflected in art. It is therefore suggested that in pursuit of a core curriculum integrating various related learning experience that is recommended in this work, a teacher should ask his class to paint the mode of life as reflected in music or dance.

Physical Education – Training of the body and mind of a learner has been the concern of educators since the ancients. Music has played a leading role in the programs designed to train the body and mind. As music and dance performance involve coordinated body movements, so they do have direct influence on the development of the body and mind. The same argument could be advanced with regard to performances of play songs.

In the Course Work there are several dance songs as well as play songs. In the sample lessons attached to the songs there are detailed and illustrated dance or play instructions appropriate for each song. Suggestions have been made in the sample lessons to the effect that such lessons should coincide with Physical Education lessons.

Since the usual practice in Uganda Primary School is to have one teacher offer instructions in all subjects in his class, so a trend toward the core curriculum integrating various related learning experiences is highly feasible.

Musicology – In Chapter V, mention has been made of sideline studies afforded by the collection of African Folk songs appearing in the Course Work. It will suffice to emphasize here that the collection is bound to enrich the study of musicology in certain fields, especially in the field of rhythm.

Rhythm is deeply rooted in the psychological grounds as a function of our bodies. It is one of several elements which all concur in creating beauty of sound. A conceptual realization of rhythm as employed in African Music is bound to enrich the music of other cultures.

Anthropology – It has already been emphasized in this work that African Music is part of the whole process of living; therefore, it should be studied as a broad human phenomenon.

As African Music forms a key position in "Man's cumulative learned behavior" or culture,[110] it has rightfully caught the attention of anthropologists to such an extent that there has emerged a branch of musical anthropologists among them.

A study of his musical traditions would throw light on the African's social environment, his historical background and political framework, as well as spiritual concepts.

History – African verbal artists have for centuries treasured historical events in poems and song. Consequently, the value of music in the reconstruction of African history is being acknowledged.

The collection of songs appearing in the Course Work contains, apart from the presence of historical songs, the whole story of man. Therefore, it offers an insight into the past and thus contributes enormously to the study of history.

Cultural Growth – The collection of songs appearing in the Course Work is representative of the rich and diverse East African cultural heritages. It has already been pointed out in this work that African tradition which surround rituals of all kinds are expressed in music, and that music is firmly entrenched in

---

110   Merriam, Alan P. The Anthropology of Music (1964). North-western University, p. 21.

the diversity of social functions found in Africa. It has also been asserted in this work that music in Africa forms part of the whole process of living.

It follows, therefore, that a study of music such as is proposed in this work is bound to promote growth and development of culture among the future generations. Also, this study is bound to mitigate against negative effects accruing from the ambivalence, among present-day schooled Africans, toward their cultural heritages.

The study proposed in this dissertation promises an education that would make the educands conscientious members of their community, rather than turn them away from the community. The study promises an education that will enable the educands to render valuable service to their community. The study promises an education that would turn the educands into good leaders of their community. Finally, the study would provide conditions in which music would become a strong constructive force in the life of the community.

Bibliography

Adam and Bjork. Education in Developing Areas. New York (1969)

Archambaut, Reginald D. (Editor). John Dewey on Education. Modern Library.

Blood, A.G. (Editor). The Fortunate Few. London: Universities' Mission to Central Africa (1954).

Brembeck, K.O. Education in Emerging Africa.

Briggs, Thomas H. Pragmatism and Pedagogy. New York: The Macmillan Company (1940).

Broady, K.O. Enriched Curriculum for Small Schools. The Small School in Action Series.

Cantor, Nathaniel. Dynamics of Learning. Buffalo: Forster and Stewart (1950).

Carrington, John F. Talking Drums of Africa. London: Carry Kingsgate Press (1949).

Coombs, Philip H. The World Educational Crises. London: Oxford University Press (1949).

Coombs, Philip H. The World Educational Crises. London: Oxford University Press (1968)

Curle, Adam. Educational Strategy for Developing Society. London: Tavistock Publication (1963).

Dewey, John. The School and Society. The University of Chicago Press (1943).

Democracy and Education. New York: Free Press (1966).

Dietz, Elizabeth Hoffmann (Warner). Musical Instruments of Africa.

Douglass, Harl R. Principles and Procedures of Curriculum Improvement. The Douglas Series in Education.

Ekundayo, Phillips. Yoruba Music; African Fusion of Speech and Music. Johannesburg: African Music Society (1953).

Eosze, Laszlo. Zoltan Kodaly: His Life and Work. London: Collect's Holdings Ltd. (1962)

Fannie, Shafted R. "Values in a World of Many Cultures." Educational Leadership 18 (May 1961).

Grant, Margaret, School Methods with Young Children; A Handbook of Teachers in Africa. London: Evans (1960).

Hall, James Husst. The Art Song. Norman: The University of Oklahoma Press (1953).

Hanson, John W. Imigination and Hallucination in African Education. Michigan State University (1967).

Hoernle, A.W. "An Outline of the Native Conception of Education in Africa." Africa, vol. IV, pp. 145-63.

Hornbostel, Eric M. von. "African Negro Music." Africa. Vol. I, No. 1 (1928).

Jones, A.M. Studies in African Music. London: Oxford University Press, (1961).

Jones, Gresford H. Uganda in Transformation. London (1926).

Jowitt, Harold. Principles of Education for African Teachers. London: Longmans, Green and Co. (1960).

Kyagambiddwa, Joseph. African Music from the Source of the Nile. New York: Frederick A. Parege (1955).

Lucas, Eric. English Traditions in East African Education. London: Oxford University Press (1959).

Mbabi-Katana, Solomon, Introduction to East African Music for Schools. Kampala: Uganda Adult Education Foundation (1967).

Songs of East Africa, Book I, London: Macmillan and Co., Ltd. (1965).

African Music for schools Bk I, Bk II and Bk III Pelican Publishers.

Music Course for Uganda, Primary I and II.

Mbuga, Stephen B.G. Church Law and Bantu Music. Schoneck-Beckenried (1963). (Nene Zeitschriff fur Missions Wissenschaft, Supplementa, 13).

Merriam, Alan Parkhurst. A Prologue to the Study of the African Arts. Yellow Springs. Ohio: Antioch Press (1961).

The Anthropology of Music. Northwestern University (1964).

Middleton, John. Myth and Cosmos. New York: Natural History Press (1967).

Moore, Clark D. and Dunbar, Ann (Editors). Africa Yesterday and Today. Bantam Books (1970).

Natanson, Rose (Brandel). The Music of Central Africa. The Hague: M. Nijhoff (1961).

Nelson, Henry B. (Editor). Basic Concepts in Music Education. Chicago: NSSE (1958).

Nketia, Kwebena, J. African Music in Ghana. Accra: Longmans (1962).

Our Drums and Drummers. Accra: Ghana Publishing House (1968).

Nyerere, Julius. Education for Self-reliance.

Parrinder, Geoffrey. African Mythology. London: The Hamlyn Publishing Group, Ltd. (1967).

Rensburg, van Patric. Education and Development in an Emerging Country. Uppsala. Scandinavia, Institute of African Studies.

Report: African Education Commission (1923-1924). London: Commonwealth Relations Office.

Report: African Education Conference (Oxford 1959). London: Commonwealth Relations Office.

Report: Advisory Committee on Native Education in British Tropical African Dependences – Parliament Papers by Command cmd 2374 – London. Commonwealth Relations Office.

Report: British and Education in the Commonwealth. London: H.M. Stationery Office, 1964.

Report: Uganda Education Commission. Entebbe (1962).

Report: International Institute for Educational Planning. Paris: 1964.

Resnick, Idrian N. Tanzania: Revolution by Education. Arusha: Longman of Tanzania (1968).

Sasnett, Martena Tenney. Educational Systems of Africa.

Trowell, Margaret and Wachsmann, K.P. Tribal Crafts of Uganda. London: Oxford University Press (1953).

Uganda: Annual Education Department Reports.

Uganda: Committee of African Education. Entebbe (1953).

Uganda: Progress Report. Entebbe (1953).

Uganda Society: Towards the New Africa. Kampala (1947).

Uganda Periodicals: Background to Uganda. Kampala: Department of Information.

Uganda (Hansard). History of Educational Thought. New York: Van Nostrand Reinhold Co. (1968).

Wachsmann, K.P. Folk Musicians in Uganda. Kampala: The Uganda Museum (1956).

Weeks, Sheldon G. Divergence in Educational Development. The Case of Kenya and Uganda. New York: Centre for Education in Africa, Teacher's College Press (1967).

Westermann, Diedrich. The African To-day. London: Oxford University Press (1934).

Willscher, Odo. Uganda, The Cradle of the Nile. Kampala (1964).